Swedish Vallhund

The Swedish Vallhund Dog Manual

Care, costs, feeding, grooming, training,
health all included.

by

Clifford Whortington

Table of Contents

Introduction

I was a farm boy. We always had dogs on the farm and I have dogs now. Dogs make wonderful pets if we care for them, spend time with them, train them, and love them. I am writing this book for those who want to know about the Swedish Vallhund as a pet.

We have more than enough dogs in our world (though we could use more Vallhunds), so I have included just a few words about breeding your Vallhund. Also, I've not talked much about 'showing' your Vallhund; I'll leave that to the experts. This book is about a slightly crazy, sweet dog who could be the best friend you've ever had – and how you could make him happy.

In the book I've called the breed Swedish Vallhund, Vallhund, SV, and Vall, with avoidance of their Swedish name: Västgötaspet.

Chapter 1: Introducing the Swedish Vallhund

If you glimpsed at the dog above standing in a few inches of grass, you might think he was a German shepherd or another large dog. Meet the Swedish Vallhund. This is a dog with a long sturdy body but very short legs. The shoulders of a Vallhund are barely a foot high. A rare breed, the Swedish Vallhund can be a lovely family pet, a working herder on the farm, a show dog, a competitor in agility trials – or all of the above.

The Vallhund may be difficult to identify at first, as the breed has so many different tail shapes and variations in coat color. The Vallhund below has the more recognizable curled tail and a grey/yellow/white coat. In this book you will learn more about the Vallhund and be able to decide if this is the dog for you.

Chapter 2: History of the Swedish Vallhund

1. The Little Viking Dog

This Swedish Vallhund (SV) existed at least 1,000 years ago as one of the small dogs favored by the Vikings. The Vikings brought the dog to Sweden in the 8th or 9th century where it became a common farm dog called the Viking Cattle Dog. The dog was used to herd cattle and as a general farm dog: it killed rats, was a good watchdog, and could almost feed itself on what it could hunt.

2. Baron von Rosen and Topsy

The breed started to die out in the early part of the 20th century, as farming methods changed. By the early 1940s, the breed had almost disappeared. Baron Bjorn von Rosen was rescuing some other Swedish dog breeds when he realized he no longer saw the little cattle dogs of his boyhood summers in southwest Sweden.

In 1942, Rosen advertised in a newspaper for good specimens of the cattle dog. A teacher, K.G. Zettersten answered the ad. The two men and Zettersten's students bicycled all over the countryside looking for dogs that were not mixed with other breeds.

At first they found four dogs, three females (Vivi, Lessi and Topsy) and one male (Mopsen) who had just one testicle. After the breed was recognized, Zettersten, a terrier judge and breeder, began to breed the cattle dogs. He and Rosen found two more bitches, Bella and Tyra. Later they found additional SVs and added them to their breeding program after the breed was recognized.

They showed these cattle dogs and their offspring throughout Sweden. In 1943, the Swedish Kennel Club recognized the dog as a separate breed. The Kennel Club commissioned Rosen to write the standard for the breed, which he did based upon Topsy's measurements. Topsy was a 12-year-old dog and may not have been bred after they found her. The first standard was for a grey dogs with stub tails and to include more color and tail options.

The Swedish Kennel Club originally named the breed Swedish Vallhund, or Swedish Herding Dog but later changed its name in 1964 to the Västgötaspet, honoring Västergötland, the province where the breed was rescued.

3. Leaving Sweden

The first known SV to leave Sweden went to Finland in 1964. The first SVs in the UK arrived during 1973 & 1974 when four dogs entered. Australia's first SV was in 1981. The first SV in the United States didn't arrive until 1985. These dogs are now a recognized breed in at least twelve countries.

The Swedish Vallhund is still a rare breed today. For example, of 177 breeds registered with the American Kennel Club, the SV ranks 147th. There are thought to be less than a thousand SV's in the US.

In Sweden, of the 70,000 dogs registered with the Swedish Kennel Club each year, only 100 are Swedish Vallhunds.

The Kennel Club (UK) registered 223,770 dogs in 2013 and only 58 were SVs.

The UK Kennel Club recognized the Swedish Vallhund as a breed in the pastoral group in 1996. The original FCI standards were approved in 1999. The American Kennel Club recognized the breed as part of the herding group in 2007.

4. Relation to Corgis

The Swedish Vallhund is often thought to be closely related to the Pembroke Welsh Corgi and Cardigan Welsh Corgi. The dogs look similar, but so far any genetic testing has not linked the Vallhund to the other breeds.

Chapter 3: Physical Description of the SV

The SV is a sturdy dog with a long solid body and short powerful legs. The dogs range from 11½ to 13½ inches (30-34 cms) high at the shoulder with females shorter than the males. The SV's body is generally 50% longer that its height. For comparison, a German shepherd dog has a body that's less than 20% longer than its height. An adult will weigh around 20-35 lbs. (9-16 kg).

1. Coat

The Vallhund has a thick waterproof coat with two layers. The top layer is of medium length, dense and coarse. The inner coat is soft and dense and has a light color. The dog will shed the winter undercoat in the spring. Colors are those of a wolf and can include white plus shades of grey, red, or yellow-brown. The coat color is called a sable pattern: a single strand of hair can have more than one type of melanin. Some hairs have dark tips with a lighter middle and a base still a different color.

A harness marking is preferred and is essential for show dogs; this is a line of a lighter color along the sides of the animal from the shoulder along the chest to elbow-height. Standards of the different breed organizations usually call for the color white not to exceed 30% of the total coat.

2. Tails

About half of SV puppies are born with no tail at all or one that will grow to a 4-inch (10 cm) stub; the other dogs have tails which range from longer thin tails to a full curled spitz-like tail. The tail variations of the SV result from the dominant stub tail gene (C189G).

None of the original four dogs had a fully fluffed-out curled tail. From photographs it appears most had stub tails. As the first breed standard written by Rosen was for a stub tail, this may have led to the practice of docking all tails that appeared in later SV puppies. Docking was outlawed in Sweden in 1989 and many breeders worldwide are now following Sweden's example.

Chapter 4: Breed Standards

1. Organizations with Standards for the SV

Breed standards for the SV have been established by several organizations. These include the Fédération Cynologique Internationale (FCI), the American Kennel Club, The United Kennel Club (USA), The Kennel Club (UK), and the Australian National Kennel Council, Ltd. Breed standards change from time to time so if you are concerned if the dog you are acquiring will meet the standard for a particular organization, you can find them on their websites.

The FCI is an organization of European and South American national groups, which use the FCI standards with minor variations.

2. "Faults"

Characteristics which would eliminate a dog from American Kennel Club competition are currently: a fluffy coat; any color other than grey, red or yellow-brown; nose not predominantly black; coat more than one-third white; any bite other than scissor. There are restrictions for height but not weight. The body has to conform to the 2:3 height/length ratio.

FCI's list of disqualifying faults include an aggressive or overly shy dog; over or undershot bite; blue eyes, one or both; hanging or semi-erect ears; long curly coat; black, white, liver brown or blue coat. Other faults for FCI that may also disqualify a dog depend upon their degree and whether the fault poses a health or welfare threat to the dog.

There is a nice description of a judge's observation of six dogs and their 'faults' at www.vastagopets.com in the section on correct anatomy. Don't forget -- an SV that does not meet breed standards is still a wonderful pet!

3. Variations in the SV's Coat

There are plenty of Swedish Vallhunds born with colors different to the kennel clubs' standards. Some are pure white, white with patches of tan, light blue and blue with splotches of color.

There is also a genetic variation within the breed, FGF5, which causes the dog to have a long outer coat much like a collie's -- soft and fluffy. The gene is recessive, so dogs with two copies of the gene have the fluffy coat. The fluffy dogs cannot compete in championship confirmation dog shows but can be registered as purebred and compete in other events.

SV breeders do not breed two fluffies but many are concerned that the fluffy could become a designer dog in the future.

Chapter 5: Traits of the Swedish Vallhund

The Swedish Vallhund is an energetic, alert dog, intelligent and eager to please.

The traits of the SV are anchored in their history. Owners of the SV describe their animals as intelligent, active, energetic, playful, agile, loving, watchful, friendly, outgoing, stubborn, strong, fearless, alert, bold, curious, obedient, loyal, even-tempered, silly, clownish, and eager to please. These attributes can be traced back to the centuries in Sweden this dog spent with families herding their grazing animals, catching vermin, and guarding their homes -- all the while being the family pet.

1. The Herder

This dog was bred to be a working herder dog that controlled a large group of animals all by itself. One farmer bragged that all he had to do in the morning was walk around a field to outline it. His dog would keep the cattle within the perimeter and return the cows to the barn when he whistled at night.

As a herding dog, it is a heeler -- a dog that herds by crouching low and nipping at the heels of its flock. The SV is agile and built low to the ground which makes it easier to dodge the kicks of its charges.

As a family pet, the instinct to be in charge and herd is still there, stronger in some animals than in others. If there is no livestock on the property, the dog may try to herd anything ... family pets, family members, visitors, joggers, bikes, cars. Some of them may still nip at the heels of people and other animals. The herding and nipping instincts can be controlled with training.

This dog needs to work and enjoys learning new things. It excels at dog agility, obedience, conformation, tracking, and Treibball competitions. In addition to regular fetch and Frisbee, the dog can learn the names of several objects to fetch on command.

2. The Watchdog

As a small watchdog the SV will bark to alert the family of anyone approaching his property. He'll bark at birds, airplanes and sometimes just to hear himself talk. Early socialization of the dog with people, other animals, and different locations is essential to reduce this 'stranger danger' habit. The dog can be trained when to bark so it doesn't become a problem.

3. The Family Pet

As a family dog the SV's personality shines. This is a friendly, playful dog, some say one with a sense of humor. Owners report that their SVs like to be with them and want to be included in everything they do. They love the outdoors but when the family go inside the home, the dog wants to be there too.

4. Don't Make Myths Come True!

You will read that the Swedish Vallhund is a hyperactive, snapping, nipping, barking dog that is a handful to manage. That it snaps at children and knocks them over, growls at strangers, and is aggressive to other dogs and cats. You'll hear that it cowers at noise and can't be taken out on city streets because it wants to herd anything it sees. All of this describes an SV whose owner has not trained and socialized the dog.

The good news: owners of 162 SVs in the Orthopedic Foundation for Animals survey reported only one aggressive dog, six timid ones, and four afraid of noise and storms.

Chapter 6: Health of the Swedish Vallhund

The Swedish Vallhund has one of the longest lifespans of all dogs, an estimated 12 to 16 years. A Kennel Club (UK) study in 2004 found only six breeds living longer. The breed can adapt to almost any climate -- although most of them love the snow. The breed is generally very healthy but does carry the risk of a few inherited diseases and some conditions common to dogs of the same shape and size.

1. Hip Dysplasia

Hip dysplasia is an inherited condition and refers to a hip's poorly formed ball and socket: the socket isn't as deep as it should be, and the ball doesn't really fit into it. This leads to arthritis, and in some dogs, total loss of cartilage, exposing nerves in the bone. Hip muscles and tendons are loose and become looser over time.

There are several different hip scoring systems. The Orthopedic Foundation of Animals (OFA)(US) has been following hip dysplasia in all dog breeds since 1974. During that time there has been a decrease in this condition, as breeders have worked to control it. For all periods 1974 to 2013, 9.6% of Swedish Vallhund's had hip dysplasia in some form (mild, moderate, or severe). But for dogs born in 2006-2010, only 8% were dysplastic.

Any animal to be bred should be x-rayed first to rule out a severe form of the condition. While the OFA formal hip score is made on 2-year-old dogs, they have been doing preliminary hip scores on puppies as young as 4 months old for breeders who are tracking their litters.

The OFA system scores the xrays using a formula that estimates how well the ball is in the socket and gives seven grades ranging from excellent to severely dysplastic. A German system is similar to the OFA but has five grades. Dogs may have to be sedated to take the x-rays.

Another US hip scoring system is the PENNHIP. This system provides the same information as the OFA but then adds an estimate of the laxity of the hip joint and a prediction of future hip problems for the dog. Dogs are anesthetized for this.

The BFV system developed in the UK looks at 9 features of the x-ray, which are graded from 0-5 or 0-6. The best hips are 0-0 (no problems with both hips, and the worst are 53-53 (both hips horrible). Dogs could need sedation or anesthesia for this test.

Potential owners should expect reports of the hips of parents and grandparents of any dog they're considering. If you have a puppy, feed it carefully, avoiding over-nutrition, which can affect the dog's growth plates in the legs. Seriously dysplastic hips may require surgery.

2. Patellar Luxation

Patella luxation, or trick knee, is seen in about 6% of the SVs. Grooves in the thigh bone, which guide the kneecap's movement, may be shallow in some dogs, allowing the kneecap to pop out. When this happens the dog pulls up lame and waits; the kneecap usually slides back in place. Exercise and maintaining trim body weight are the best preventives of this condition; serious cases may require surgery.

3. Progressive Retinal Atrophy (PRA)

The Canine Eye Registration Foundation (CERF) found less than 2% of SVs were suspected of having PRA. This disease is caused by rods and cones in the retina losing their ability to react to light. The dog first has night blindness, then lowered vision in daylight. In some dog breeds there are genetic tests for PRA. In the SV there appear to be many genes involved and the genetic research continues. It seems so far that PRA is relatively mild in SVs.

4. Cataracts

Some online health summaries of SVs report cataracts as a problem condition of the breed. I found no studies to support this.

One US study (Kamaromy, 2005) of SVs of 34 dogs found tiny cataracts in 15% of them. The author did not know of any dogs in the US blinded by cataracts but thought breeders should not mate two dogs if both had the tiny cataracts.

In The Orthopedic Foundation for Animals' survey of owners of 162 dogs: only three dogs were reported with eye problems; one with juvenile cataracts, which often disappear with treatment.

5. Cryptorchidism

Cryptorchidism, or undescended testicle, is an inherited condition in about 8% of male dogs. Mopsen, the male dog which began the SV breed, had this condition. Dogs with this condition should not be bred and do not compete in show trials. Removal of any undescended testicle is recommended by most veterinarians to prevent testicular cancer. Dogs with a retained undescended testicle are thirteen times more likely to get the cancer.

6. Back Problems

Because of its long back, the SV is prone to have later arthritic changes. The best prevention is to maintain a healthy body weight.

7. Cleft Conditions

The dogs have a risk of having puppies with cleft palate and neural tube defects such as spina bifida.

Chapter 7: Should You Own Any Breed of Dog?

Many dog-owning stories begin with "Aren't they cute!" and are followed with a quick decision to buy or adopt the cute puppy or dog. Unfortunately, many of these dogs are later surrendered to a shelter. In the US, people bring an estimated 3 to 6 million dogs to shelters every year. (Shelters aren't required to report their census.)

Before you acquire any dog it might be worthwhile to read the shelter studies published by The National Council on Pet Population Study and Policy. They studied the reasons dogs were surrendered to a shelter. Reason #1 was the owner's moving and Reason #2 was the dog's behavior. Sadly, about half of all surrendered dogs had been owned for only a year or less. Only 4% of the dogs had received formal obedience training.

So. Are you about to move? Can you be sure you will move to a place where dogs are welcome? Are they really welcome where you are living now?

Dogs, especially puppies, need obedience training. Read about the efforts needed to train a puppy, to be consistent, firm. Can you and your family do this? Group classes run an hour a week for six to eight weeks for puppies and then there are further obedience classes depending upon the dog. Be honest, will you spend the time?

And cost. Some people take a dog home and just think of the cost of dog food and flea powder. Estimates of the cost of the first year of a dog's life range from $500 to $5,000 (300-3000£). Annual costs for subsequent years run from $300-$2,500 (180-1500£). This is without any extraordinary health problem with the dog. Are you ready for this?

Are you away from home a lot? Work night and day? Travel? Have unscheduled weekends away from home? Can someone take care of the dog or will you need to board it?

Just checking. If you're not sure you can take care of a dog, please don't get one. Try a cat ... they're easier.

Chapter 8: Should You Get a Swedish Vallhund?

1. Visit One

It would be nice if you could actually meet a Swedish Vallhund before deciding to get one. If this is not possible, spend a lazy afternoon watching videos online. There is a short list of my favorites in the appendix but there are dozens more -- it is a pleasant way to see the personality and vitality of this special little dog.

2. Do Your Research

Research the breed seriously. This dog may live 15 years. If you get the dog as a puppy, how you treat the dog from day one onward will shape both the dog's life and your life with the dog.

Many of the SV societies, breeders, and owners warn that an SV puppy should not be the dog for a first time dog owner. Or they suggest that a first-time dog owner should have an adult Vallhund that's already trained. I wouldn't let this discourage determined new owners from having a SV puppy as long as they truly understand the breed and are willing to devote the time and effort needed to raise it properly. But I do think that someone who has never had a dog before and who would have to leave the dog alone most of the day should probably not have a Vallhund puppy.

Also, re-homing an adult Swedish Vallhund will take time and effort as well. A notice from a breeder that a two-year-old SV was available warned that it would take four to six months to fully settle the dog in its new home.

This dog is a working herding dog and a watchdog breed. As a herder, it wants to work, be active. The watchdog wants to protect its family and bark prey away. Some of these instincts, if strong in the puppy, need to be dampened early. If not used for herding, the nipping can be reduced through training. Similarly, the dog can be trained to give one or two alerting barks when someone approaches the property, not bark its head off. Fortunately, the SV is an intelligent dog and takes well to training.

But the SV is also an intelligent dog who may become easily bored. The more talents the dog learns, the happier it'll be.

3. Do You Have the "Right" Home?

Ideally the SV would love to live with an owner and twelve children, who all love dogs and are always at home and the dog has five other SVs to play with in a big fenced yard. But none of these conditions are essential. The SV doesn't need vigorous exercise, just a good run every day and a walk can do. The dog can be raised in an apartment by a single owner who works outside the home -- as long as the owner spends lots of time with the dog at other times. The SV does love to sit and be petted. This dog is not for someone who cannot take the dog outside for walks (or have someone else do it every day).

One good thing about the Swedish Vallhund's short legs is that it can get some of its needed exercise just by running through a house or apartment. (And don't get this dog if that just made you shiver.)

Dog parks and group dog training can take the place of a built-in dog family. The SV can be trained for agility, tracking, herding, Treibball, and obedience competitions. If not trained for competitions, the SV will be just as happy playing soccer with its human friends or being taught silly tricks. Owners can play fetch with them: they learn the words of several objects and fetch them on command. In Sweden, SVs have been trained to hunt truffles; and in England SVs have been trained as retrieving bird dogs. SVs also make good therapy and search & rescue dogs.

In later chapters on early care of the puppy and training I'll provide the details of socialization and training. It is important for the puppy to see many adults, children, other animals, and to visit many strange places and hear noises.

4. Children

I don't know how to say this kindly. If you haven't trained your children, don't take on this dog. At least don't get a puppy. The puppy's bones aren't developed and can be easily hurt by rough play.

Chapter 9: Can You Afford a Swedish Vallhund?

Estimates of the cost of caring for the SV will vary widely. Variations will depend upon where you live, the choices you make for fancier products, and costs to make your home the best place for the dog. You can also reduce costs by buying some things from resale shops.

I've separated my discussion of expenses into possible first year expenses; then subsequent annual expenses, followed by potential expenses (without figures – just to discuss things that can happen when owning a dog). I've not included in these estimates costs to fly your adult dog on trips with you, boarding/day care, breeding, competitions, and end-of-life expenses, but have discussed them in their chapters.

1. First Year Expenses

First year expenses can range from $1,120-$12,465 (675-7500£).

I'm not trying to frighten you, but... The lower estimate assumes you have access to low-cost veterinary care. The higher estimate includes a pricey dog and international shipping, plus fencing the yard and other things. But please use the cost categories to make your own estimate before acquiring a Vallhund.

Acquisition of the dog: $0-$1,500 (0-900£).
The zero cost estimate is if someone gives the dog to you. Remember, though, if the dog is a gift you may have to pay for vaccines, microchips and other services included in a shelter adoption or purchase from a breeder.

If you find the SV at a shelter or rescue organization you could pay anywhere from $50-$250 (30-150£) or more. Usually the shelter fee includes spaying/neutering the pet.

Breeders generally charge from $500 to $1,500 (300-900£). This may include registration of the pedigree, health certifications, socialization, worming, vaccinations, microchipping, help after sale, and if the dog does not work out with your family ... transportation back to the breeder.

Transport: $0-2,000 (0-1200£)
It would be ideal for you to meet your puppy before you buy it. This may not be possible if the breeder lives too far away or even in a different country.
Breeders are accustomed to air shipping dogs to their new owners. There are also land-based pet courier services that travel within the US, Canada, Europe and Australia/New Zealand.
Cost depends upon the dog's size, distance travelled, quarantine issues, and health certificates needed.

Microchip: $0-$50 (0-30£)
Dogs from a breeder will probably be microchipped already. Other dogs may not be. The cost is for implanting the chip into the dog and a lifetime service to locate you if the dog is found. Do remember to notify the service of any change of address

Annual city/town registration: $5-50 (3-30£) per year

Fence for the yard: Cost depends upon size ($0-3,000; 0-1800£)
It is ideal to have a yard where the dog can run and play. Your Vallhund will take a rubber ball and play a long lively game of soccer all by itself. (See YouTube: Swedish Vallhund footballing legend!)

You also may need additional fencing just to protect flower gardens in the yard or to fence off spas and other attractions.
If you need to add a fence it should be at least five feet (1.5 m) high, these little dogs can jump and climb!
Costs may run to $25 per linear foot or more. (Or around 50£ per meter.)

Housetraining: $150 (90£)
This is for puppy pads, a low plastic pan slightly larger than the dog to place a puppy pad, and a puppy playpen.

The costs would be about the same for a crate, if you choose this method to housetrain.

Bed: $50 (30£)
Look for washable covers and waterproof interiors. After your dog is older, it will need another bed that offers good orthopedic support for its long back.

Water bowl and food dish: $30 (18£)
Buy adult-sized dishes, one-quart for water, and one pint for food. Stainless steel dishes weighted to avoid tipping over are best. Buy separate dishes.

First aid kit & supplies: $50-$100 (30-60£)

Collar and leashes: $40 (24£)
A simple nylon collar and light leash is all you really need at first. Later you'll want a long lead for fun outside.

Safety harness for your car: $20 (12£)

Small carrying case for your puppy: $35 (21£)

Toys: $50-$200 (30-120£)
Your dog will be spending some time alone and needs something to play with: a bored dog can be a destructive dog.

Your breeder may know if your puppy prefers hard, soft, or rope toys. A ball, a hollow toy for putting treats inside, and another hard or soft toy will get you started. (Customers complain that manufactured treats fall out of the hollow toys, but homemade extra dry treats, peanut butter or frozen treats work well.)

If you are going to be away at work, you may want to indulge in automated toys such as iFetch, which can "play" with your dog.

Grooming tools: $40 (24£)
Get a good brush, nail clippers, toothpaste, and fingertip toothbrush.

Food, treats and chew bones: $400 (240£) per year
Food cost will depend upon what your breeder and veterinarian recommend. Chapter 25 contains a discussion of different types of food available for dogs.

Flea & Tick Control, Heartworm prevention: $70-$300 (40-180£) per year

Dogs can get a pesky skin allergy just from the skin's reaction to flea saliva. They can get several viral and bacterial diseases from flea and tick bites. Dogs get worms from eating fleas as they groom themselves. It makes every bit of common sense to provide your dog with a regular flea and tick control program.

Many owners use a monthly drug applied to the dog's skin. The medication is supposed to last a month but in 'flea season' many owners have observed they only last three weeks. Other owners live in areas where powders and bath products are effective. Talk with your veterinarian to pick the schedule and drug best suited for your dog.

Heartworm prevention is an issue wherever there are mosquitoes. If a dog gets heartworm it can cost $500-$1,200 (300-725£) to treat. Before some heartworm medications are started the dog must be tested, which would add $40-50 (24-30£) to the estimate. Your veterinarian can help you decide which medications are safe for your dog.

Veterinary Costs: (excluding spay/neuter cost): ($80-$500; 50-300£)
Cost of veterinary visits will vary widely depending upon where you live. The first year there's a minimum of two visits for completing vaccinations. Charges usually are higher in larger

cities, but cities are often where there may be more low-cost options. ($40 - $200; 24-120£)

Vaccines. The cost of vaccines will depend upon where you live – both because of community cost & available low-cost clinics and the number of diseases you need vaccines for. ($40-$300;24-180£)

Spay/neutering: ($0-$300; 0-180£)

These costs will vary by locality. It's worthwhile to research fees in your area. Many shelter and rescue organizations offer very low cost or free spay & neuter clinics.

There is an additional cost for testicular implants.

Dog training and sports "clubs" ($100-$1,000; 60-600£)

Many have an annual fee of about $100 (60£) and charges of about $25 (15£) for weekly classes or sport training sessions. At a minimum, go through a 6-week class as part of socializing your puppy and use a service without annual fee. If your dog loves the challenge, I recommend weekly training sessions of some sort, either through a "club" or with friends in the park.

Pet Insurance: $22-$52 (13-31£) per month or higher ($0-$2,700; 0-1630£)

Pet insurance protects you against a financial crisis from an accident or illness. If your SV develops a hip or knee problem that needs surgery, can you easily pay the $1,500-$6,000 (905-3620£) bill? Blogs of SV owners are filled with stories of serious injuries happening when these active dogs step in gopher holes or fall off steps and rocks.

Pet insurance is still rarely used in the US; maybe 5% of dogs are insured. By contrast, in Sweden, health insurance for dogs started in 1924 and now an estimated 80% of owners have it. In the UK, at least 25% have pet insurance; in Canada, 9%.

Pet insurance has as many options as human medical insurance. Some high-end policies will pay all veterinarian bills as they come in and up to a certain level, without any co-pay or deductible, lower cost policies have higher deductibles and lower annual maximums.

Examples for 2014 include a $22 (13£) per month policy for accidents and illnesses, which pays 80% of the bill after a $500 (300£) annual deductible with a $5,000 (3000£) annual limit. A $52 (31£) per month policy still pays 80% of the bill but reduces the deductible to $200 (120£) and increases the annual limit to $10,000 (6000£). There are riders for many of the policies which cover preventive care.

Some puppies will come from the breeder with a few weeks of pet insurance.

2. Expenses after the First Year

Annual expenses from the second year until well into your dog's senior years can range from $550 to $6,360 (330-3840£).

- License ($5-$50;3-30£)
- Dog pads (high number is for apartment dwellers) ($0-$450;0-270£)
- Bed (will have to replace from time to time) ($0-$90;0-55£)
- Collars/harness (training will change) ($20-$30;12-18£)
- Toys ($20-$50;12-30£)
- Food ($400;240£)
- Fleas/Tick/Worm meds ($70-$300;42-180£)
- Visits to veterinarian (the low number is for one well-dog visit to clinic; the $854 is average cost in US. ($20-$850;15-515£)
- Vaccines ($15-$100;9-60£)
- Supplements ($0-40;0-24£)
- Dog training and/or sports "clubs" ($0-$1,300;0-785)
- Dog insurance ($0-$2,700;0-1630£)

3. Potential Expenses

Homeowners Insurance:
This is something for you to check.
The SV puppy is prone to nipping, especially the legs of running children; the adult SV will do this also if not trained.
In the US, the Centers for Disease Control estimated there were almost 5 million dog bites a year and that these cost victims a billion dollars each year. While insurance companies so far pay for less than 20,000 of these injuries, they responded by either not including dog bite coverage or severely reducing it. Also, many apartment dwellers, especially younger folks, do not even have homeowners insurance.

Attorney costs:

This is another thing to think about; mostly to think about the value of training your Vallhund.

Dog biting, car chasing, and uncontrolled barking can land you in legal trouble.

You may also want an attorney to check any contract you sign with a breeder.

Other costs Owners Didn't Plan On
The American Pet Products Association surveys dog owners every year. For 2013 they reported on some unforeseen costs of dog owners. These included:
Ruined dog beds that weren't waterproof, chewed shoes, IPhones, and other household items
High veterinary bills from injuries, accidents, allergies
Higher security deposits followed by lost security deposits on apartments and rented houses.

Chapter 10: Finding your Swedish Vallhund

The Swedish Vallhund is a rare breed. Chances are you'll have to do some research to find a purebred Swedish Vallhund. Ask your veterinarian, if you have one. Another place to start is the club associated with the breed in your country -- they will have lists of breeders. Start with these breeders and talk with them; they may know of additional good breeders who are not listed or of someone who has to give up an older dog.

Often when you find a breeder you like, you will be screened, and -- if the breeder is satisfied you will take good care of her dog -- placed on a waiting list for a puppy. Some have waited two years or more for their Valls. You will be asked your preference for the sex of a puppy, its tail type, or coat color, but you may not be able to get your preferences.

WARNING: If you do an Internet search and find a puppy for sale, double-check the website. There are several online virtual games that involve managing kennels, buying and selling dogs. Two of these are Furry Paws and Showdog.com.

1. Swedish Vallhund Clubs

The Swedish Vallhund Club of America lists 22 breeders in the US. The UK Vallhund organization lists 5 breeders. The Canadian club lists 6 breeders. The combined website for Australia/New Zealand provides announcements of both recent litters as well as upcoming births, which is helpful. It also gives a list of over 150 breeders worldwide. There are an estimated ten to twelve active SV breeders in Australia/New Zealand.

2. Rescue dogs

Adult dogs are occasionally available through rescue operations of the SV clubs. The Swedish Vallhund Club of America, for example, has a formal rescue program. This program involves a three-week fostering period for diagnosis of any medical and behavioral problems, groomed, and spayed or neutered. For the applicant, there is a required fee, completed application form, interview, and home visit. There is a waiting list but no SVs have needed rescue from the national programs in 2012 or 2013.

3. Pounds/Shelters

About 25% of shelter dogs are purebred, but as the Vallhund is rare among purebred dogs it will also be rarely found in shelters. Many shelters have fine screening programs so it is not impossible to find a healthy SV there.

4. Vallhund owners

You may be able to locate an SV by joining breed groups on Facebook or other social sites and blogs. At a minimum, you'll find names to research. There is a UK Swedish Vallhunds group, a Swedish Vallhunds in America group, and Swedish Vallhund Club. Inc. NZ chat page on Facebook. And don't forget the Swedish websites -- Google is amazing and can translate almost everything. The principal Swedish sites for Valls are Svenska vallhundsklubben (www.SVAK.se) and Svenska Kennelklubben (www.SKK.se).

Also, as you research breeders they may steer you to owners of the dog in your area who may have leads of available puppies and dogs.

Chapter 11: The Breeder and You

Some people shudder to think of paying for a good purebred dog. They don't know that a good breeder, through selective breeding of dogs of known pedigrees, can save you money in the long run. Consider the $500 to $1,500 (300-905£) paid for a breeder's dog against the $3,000 to $10,000 (1810-6035£) to diagnose and treat just the two potential SV hip and knee conditions.

1. Good Breeders Will Question Your Ability to Care for Their Dog

A good breeder will invite and answer your questions. A good breeder will also be very concerned whether you will make the right owner for her dog. In the appendix there is a detailed form one breeder uses to screen potential owners. Below is a short item from a breeder published on Dogzonline concerning a two-year old SV, which demonstrates the breeder's concern and intent to find the right owner for her dog:

"Barahwolfe Swedish Vallhunds have, available to the right home, a two-year-old bitch. 'Blossom' is house trained, excellent with children and is an attractive young dog. She has quite dark facial features, and ears.

We are seeking a suburban type home, fully fenced with knowledgeable dog people. Swedish Vallhunds can take 4-6 months to fully settle with their owners when they are rehomed at this age. She would fit well where there are other dogs, or where people are home often.

We are not keen to entertain a home where everyone works full time and she is alone all day. She is used to being an inside dog, but would learn to manage sleeping outdoors.

She is currently in Otago and we would prefer that she remain in the South Island, although for the right people this is negotiable.

Blossom is fully papered, and available to right home on the NZKC register. She is wormed, vaccinated, healthy and vet checked."

2. What Good Breeders Give You

Good breeders work to provide you with a healthy puppy having a temperament to best suit your family and which has been:

- Dewormed, vaccinated, and checked by a veterinarian before release
- Raised in a home and socialized with other animals, children, men and women.
- Exposed to loud and sudden noises.
- Certified that both parents are without serious genetically-transmitted hip, knee, and eye conditions

and they will provide ...

- Pedigree papers showing three or more generations and be registration in the breeder's country as purebred
- A guarantee that the puppy can be returned if a serious genetic condition appears within a given time - usually two years
- Information of any diseases or conditions in their bloodlines
- Information about any quirks your dog may have and how to handle them
- Guarantee to take the puppy back if you can't keep it. (The breeder pays for transportation costs; you don't get any refund).
- A puppy kit with written information about how to care for your dog
- If you're picking the puppy up at the breeders, a few days of puppy food and details about how it likes its food -- schedule, amount each time, warm water on kibble, etc.
- The puppy's chew toy
- A towel with heavy scent of the mother

- A promise to be there if you need any suggestions for caring for your dog
- Any words the dog already knows; And any commands it already follows
- Advice, and perhaps co-ownership for training your dog for competitions and for breeding

3. Understanding the Breeder's Investment in Your Pup

Most SV breeders are in love with their dogs and dedicated to maintaining the vigor of the breed. Don't forget the costs a good breeder experiences in raising a puppy which include:

- stud fees
- health & genetic testing
- vaccinations, worming of the pup and the breed stock
- microchipping
- feeding of puppies for a short while plus full time care of breed stock
- adding new dogs to the bloodline
- veterinary costs for puppy exam plus care of breed stock
- registration costs of puppies and breed stock
- transportation fees
- cost of caring for returned dogs and other cost from guarantees
- after sale services, communication/hand holding
- socialization time

4. Questions for the Breeder

As you are doing your research, refine your list of questions to ask breeders. Everyone will have a different focus and many such lists are available online. In addition to meeting the expectations listed above, are some questions to get you started:

- Can you visit the breeder, see how the dogs are raised, see the parents?

- If you can't visit, are the dogs available on Skype or FaceTime?

- Are the puppies raised in the house? With kids? Cats?

- Will there be any extra charges in addition to the purchase price, such as caring for the dog an extra week or two?

- How many litters do your bitches have?

- Do you breed just Swedish Vallhunds?

- Do you require spay/neutering? If yes, is there a contract or co-ownership required?

- May I have copies of any guarantees, warranties, contracts, or agreements you use?

- If I pay the deposit to reserve a puppy and later change my mind, is the deposit refundable?

Chapter 12: Choosing Your Swedish Vallhund

Some of the decisions you'll make before and after you bring your Vallhund home include:

1. Male or female?

If you plan to spay or neuter your pet there will be little difference. The females are a little smaller and some say more independent, cat-like. Males are bigger and some say more active and more eager to please. Females will be more expensive to fix unless you have a free clinic in your area.

If you're not spaying the dog, there is the twice-yearly two or three week period when she's in heat and acts strange, is messy, and needs to be kept away from intact male dogs.

If not neutering the dog, they will chase after intact females and get into dogfights if they get off the leash. People looking for show dogs may tilt toward a male dog, as they historically have done better in shows.

Generally, I would recommend that you find a good breeder, explain your lifestyle and leave it in the breeder's hands to match you with a good puppy.

2. Age of Puppy

Breeders usually release puppies between 8 and 9 weeks old. This is the best time for you to bring the puppy home. There is a critical period between birth and 16 weeks when the puppies learn what's safe in its world. Some say that the dog should meet at least 100 people during that time. It should also ride in cars, go in crowds, meet other dogs and cats and hear every machine you can find. This meeting & touring process is called socialization and can determine the success of the dog's life with you.

If the puppy is kept at home alone with one or two adults living quietly with just a TV for noise, it will learn that this is his world and everything and everyone else is foreign, strange, and to be feared -- bringing out anxiety and aggression in the dog.

3. One or two?

Your Vallhund would love another dog to live with. I wouldn't recommend bringing two puppies home at once though. First, it would be a handful -- especially if this is your first SV. But more important, if you brought two puppies home at the same time, they would bond more with each other than with you.

It would be best to introduce the second dog after a year or two. And the second dog would do best if it were of a different sex.

4. Sight Unseen?

If you found a breeder you really like but they live too far away for you to visit, should you still consider getting a puppy sight unseen?

Given that there won't be that many dogs available to you, you can still "meet" the dog on Skype or FaceTime. Many import their Valls from another country. At a minimum, most breeders post photos of their dogs on their websites.

Chapter 13: Grooming

1. Coat

Your Vallhund is an easy dog to groom. No fancy clipping – even for "dog shows" the coat is not trimmed except for hair around the foot pads.

Some say the Vall's coat is made of Teflon – dirt simply rolls off. If you're out in rain and mud, just use a dry towel to wipe your pup off when you come in. This dog doesn't even need a bath very often – when to bathe depends upon where you live and what your Vall gets up to. I'd say only bathe if he gets into something messy, smelly, or dangerous – and if that doesn't happen, maybe twice a year. When you do give him a bath, use gentle dog soap and rinse and rinse and rinse. You don't want to take away the dog's protective oils. Also, make sure you put cotton balls in his ears to keep them dry.

Usually brush the dog two or three times a week with a firm bristle brush and a slicker brush or undercoat rake. The only complaints of owners usually focus upon the times in spring and autumn when Valls shed. Their undercoat is composed of very fine hairs and if allowed to shed at will, your house will be covered from wall to wall. During these times, just brush your Vall every day. Occasionally clip the hairs on the dog's feet.

When you brush your dog, brush first against the grain so you see what lies beneath – fleas, burrs, skin irritations. Give the dog's body a good skin exam every week.

2. Teeth

In addition to providing dental treats and nubby toys to reduce tartar, you need to clean your Vall's teeth. Ideally, you'll do this every day – but three or four times a week will help prevent soft tartar from hardening. Just as for humans, eventually your dog will need professional cleaning from time to time. The greater your success with establishing regular brushing, the less frequent this will have be.

And start from Day 2 – you'll be busy on Day 1! If you do this regularly, your dog will grow to love it. Using your "Good Dog" voice, get down on the floor and just rub your fingers over your Vall's front teeth. Don't let him bite. Just spend a minute or two rubbing as far into his mouth as you can. Dip your finger in chicken broth if you have some around.) Do this for a few days and when he's used to it, try some dog toothpaste. (Never use human toothpaste.) Have your dog lick the toothpaste off your finger, then do the rubbing again.

There are flavored toothpastes – experiment with different ones to find one he really loves. Start with the finger brushes; later use the dog toothbrushes with handles. Try to get at the areas at the back, and don't brush too hard. Report any excess redness or bleeding to your vet.

If your dog gets impatient and wants to mouth you, let him bite onto a hard toy and hold his muzzle – this will give you room to brush behind the toy.

Once your SV is used to having his teeth cleaned you may try going to an electric toothbrush. They make them for dogs – you want a soft bristle – the ones with batteries seem to work best. It helps to see it done. There are plenty of videos on YouTube such as "Cleaning dog teeth with electric toothbrush – Honey the Great Dane".

3. Toenails

Why do you have to cut your dog's nails? Dogs walk on their toes. If a dog's nails are too long, it causes pain in the nail and shifts the angle of his foot when he walks, leading to long-term damage. It's especially important to keep your Vall's nails trimmed if he's playing agility sports and needs to turn and twist.

So if you hear a "click" on the floor when your dog walks across it, his nails definitely need cutting. But it would be better for him if you'd trim nails before they get to the "click" stage. Also, you need to keep an eye on the dew claws – these are usually well off the ground and are vestigial "thumbs" and "big toes". These need trimming to avoid their becoming ingrown nails.

On Day 2 with your new puppy or dog, start examining your dog's feet. Get him used to you handling them. At first you can hold him in your lap, but you also want to train him to lie on his side, as this will be how you do it later so you'll have access to all four feet at once.

Your goal is to trim the nail but not bite into the quick where blood vessels and nerves cause pain and bleeding. Many people use nail clippers – either strong scissor-like tools or ones called guillotine clippers, which have a hole that you stick the nail through to guide the cut.

Other groomers and owners are now using dremmels, which are rotary tools with small rotating sandpaper heads; some of these are compact and cordless.

Whichever tool you use, start by shaving or smoothing off just a tiny bit of nail each time. If your Vall has light nails you'll be able to see the darker quick. The dremmel is less likely to splinter a dry nail. If using manual clippers, use a nail file to smooth a clipped nail if it's ragged or splintered.

Most dogs don't like having their nails done. To make a good beginning, first get him used to you just handling his feet. Then, when you start clipping or sanding, give him a treat after each toe. If using a dremmel, get the dog used to the noise for a few days before you try using it. Don't press the nail down onto the sandpaper – touch it lightly – and do it for just a second or two at a time. Usually you just have to do the front feet.

It's important when he's a puppy to keep his nails in check. If allowed to grow long, the quick also grows long which makes caring for nails more difficult in the future. If you should nick the quick it hurts the dog and bleeds quite a bit. Apply styptic pen or powder and hold a gauze against the nail until the bleeding stops. (The styptic chemical also hurts.)

There are a number of free videos online. One rather humorous one is "How to Clip Dog Nails – Tips from the Dog Training Guys (K9-1). This particular video nicely demonstrates the angle of the cut to aim for. The graphic below shows their point: you want to cut the tip of the nail in the direction of the arrow, not a vertical cut across the nail. (The circle is the foot; the banana is the nail.)

4. Ears

The Swedish Vallhunds are prone to dirty ears and ear infections. Every week inspect your Vall's ears and clean them gently. Do not use cotton-tipped swabs. Moisten (don't drown) simple gauze squares with the ear cleaner preferred by your veterinarian, or use dog ear wipes.

Until you are used to your dog, I advise looking at his ears, use wipes to clean the area you can see, and then have your veterinarian check to see if you need to do more. She may want you to put cleaning drops into the ears, massage them, and then clean them out with gauze squares from time to time.

You don't want to irritate the ears and you don't want to poke anything too far into the ear canal. You also don't want to use anything harsh like alcohol or undiluted hydrogen peroxide.

Don't let the dog get water in his ears. If he does, fold his ears back and blot with gauze squares. Leave his ears folded back until they're dry. There are ear drying gels and powders but don't use them without your veterinarian's okay.

5. Anal Glands

I put anal glands in the grooming section, as I want to make sure you don't have a groomer or other person who thinks it's a normal grooming procedure to express your Vall's anal glands on a regular basis.

When you first get your pup or dog, take a good look at his anus while you are grooming him. And continue to inspect this area regularly. By knowing what it looks like when everything is fine and dandy, you'll be a better reporter to your veterinarian if anything goes awry.

Dogs of both sexes have anal glands just inside the rectum at four and eight o'clock. These glands release pheromones – the dog's signature smell. The glands release a smelly substance when the dog passes a firm stool. This is why dogs greet each other by smelling their butts and are so anxious to investigate each other's stools.

Usually dogs have no problem with their anal glands unless they have frequent loose stools. Then the anal glands expand making the dog uncomfortable. When dogs have discomfort around their anus they can nip and tug at it and at their tail, won't stay sitting down, and some do that scooting across the floor thing that makes people laugh.

Some people immediately decide the anal glands are the problem and need to be expressed. The problem is that if expressed too frequently, the structure of the glands can be altered and no longer operate normally.

The dog's squirrelly behavior could be caused by itching or pain and have nothing to do with the anal gland. Anal itching is common from food allergies, environmental allergies, and tapeworms, or he could have other problems.

If his stools have been soft or he's had too frequent diarrhea, solve that problem right away.

Meanwhile try relieving the condition by holding cold towels (wet cloths kept in the freezer) or massage with warm towels under his tail. Look for signs of tapeworm – they release eggs which when dry look like rice embedded in the dog's hair.

Is his anus swollen? Redder? Call your veterinarian. Stools are fine but dog still has a problem? Call your veterinarian.

Chapter 14: Spay & Neuter?

You may not have total control over the decision to spay or neuter your Swedish Vallhund.

Shelters usually spay or neuter dogs before they release them; while others require a deposit that they refund after the spay/neuter procedure.

Some US cities have mandatory spay/neuter laws. The cities often exclude show & competition dogs, professional breeders, guide dogs and police dogs from the law. Several states are studying these laws but none have been enacted.

If you've purchased the SV for a pet, the contract with your breeder will probably include your promise to spay/neuter your dog. Some breeders also maintain co-ownership of the dog until proof of spay/neuter procedure: this prevents your registering the pedigree of any resulting litters.

If you plan to show or breed an SV, you may not be able to buy the dog outright from a breeder. Many breeders will instead insist upon a co-ownership contract. This gives the breeder the right to review the genetics of any proposed mating. These co-ownership contracts for show dogs often include the breeder's right to say how the dog will be raised, fed, and shown. These contracts maintain the effort of breeders to maintain healthy genetics of the breed. Litters from a co-owned dog cannot be registered without both parties agreement.

You cannot exhibit spayed or neutered pets in dog confirmation shows but they can compete in all other competitions: agility, rally obedience, tracking, herding, field trials, earthdog, etc.

If you do have choice about whether to spay or neuter your SV, do not hurry to do so. Studies have shown that if the surgery is performed too early, bone and ligaments do not develop well and the immune system is affected.

The Orthopedic Foundation for Animals found in a survey of SVs that had been spayed or neutered, only 1.5% of the dogs and 0.9% of the bitches were spayed or neutered at ages 0-6 months.

There are articles about the negative effects of spaying or neutering but none specific to the SV. The general articles note that one side effect is an increased tendency toward obesity: a warning for you not to overfeed your SV friend.

A 2008 literature review by Root-Kuntritz on the AKC website concluded that spaying should be delayed until after six months and before the dog's first heat.

Root-Kuntritz made no similar blanket recommendation for the age at which dogs should be neutered as some breeds are susceptible to cancers and other conditions, which are higher in neutered dogs. Knee injuries/problems were the only serious condition on her list which is common to the SV; this increased risk can be reduced if the dog is neutered after six months of age; some breeders recommend not neutering a Vallhund until his bones are fully formed at 18-20 months.

1. Neuter

Benefits of neutering include:

- Dogs live longer; although incidence of some cancers are increased
- Eliminates testicular cancer; reduces some benign prostate conditions and hernias
- Reduces mounting behavior and urine spraying
- Reduces male to male dog aggression
- Reduces urge to flee & roam
- Reduced cost of licensure
- Birth control; genetic control of the breed

Downside of neutering which may affect the SV:

- Increased tendency of obesity
- Ligament problems; uneven bone growth
- Increase in hypothyroidism

2. Spay

Benefits of paying include:

- Birth control; genetic control of the breed
- Avoid erratic behavior and mess when dog in heat
- Decrease in breast cancer
- Eliminate diseases of ovaries and uterus
- Avoid confinement during heat
- Lower licensing fees

Downside of spaying:

- There is some risk from the surgery
- Increased tendency for obesity
- If done too young, urinary problems
- Cost of procedure (offset by medical expenses avoided)

Chapter 15: Getting Ready for Your Swedish Vallhund

If this is your first dog, you have some things to do before the puppy comes.

1. Where Will the Puppy Live in the House?

- The kitchen or family room is usually the place for this.

- Decide where in the house the puppy can live until fully housetrained and buy any equipment and supplies needed. This may include a crate or playpen for when the puppy is alone and gates to limit pup's access to the rest of the house when the puppy is out and about.

- Also any stairs need to be off limits until the puppy's bones are stronger.

- Make sure the puppy can't get at plants, drapes, electric or telephone cords. Nothing should be on the floor when the puppy is out except its own toys. Make sure household chemicals, paint, medicines etc. are locked away or otherwise not accessible to the puppy.

- Later, when the puppy is housetrained, you have to repeat the puppy proofing wherever it can go in the house: See Chapter 16.

2. Puppy-proof the Yard.

- Check the fence for escape routes and plug any gaps.

- Scour the yard for anything the dog can chew or choke on. Your Vall will try to eat pebbles and sticks.

- Block access to pool or spa.

- Check for holes in the ground, a puppy's legs can be hurt badly by stepping into one.

- Let the children help with this.

3. Veterinarian

If you don't have a veterinarian, get one and make an appointment, usually within 3 days after you bring the puppy home.

4. The Kids

If you have children, start training them before the puppy comes. Let them know they will not be allowed alone with the puppy until they can handle it properly. Let them see videos of puppies being trained. Discuss what they can do in the puppy's first weeks.

5. Classes

Explore your community for puppy classes. They will have rules about the number of vaccinations needed before you can participate. Your veterinarian will also have an opinion on when your puppy can be with other dogs.

6. Here Fido?

Think about your dog's name. For purebred dogs this is their "calling name".

Dogs seem to respond best to short names, one or two syllables. Since this is a Swedish Vallhund you might consider a Viking or Swedish name. (The list of websites in the appendix has addresses for these names.) Also research the early Vallhunds and their names; some of these are in articles at www.konnunkodon.fi/en.

If you are getting the dog from a breeder, the breeder will probably have given the pup its registered name.

7. Shop

Go shopping for essentials. (See Chapter 9) For food, check with breeder and buy the brand of puppy food your pup is eating.

8. Schedule Vacation Time

If possible, arrange to have an adult always at home with the puppy at least for its first week.

Chapter 16: Puppy & Dog Proofing Your House

As your puppy and later, your dog, earns access to areas of the house beyond its initial confinement area, continue to remove any hazards to the dog or anything you do not want chewed or broken.

Be aware that your Swedish Vallhund puppy will want to touch, sniff, taste, investigate and closely inspect every electrical cord, every closet, every nook and cranny of your home and everything you may have left lying about on the floor.

Power cords are in just about every room in the home and to a teething puppy -- these may look like irresistible, fun, chew toys. Make sure that you tuck all power cords securely out of your puppy's reach or put them inside a chew-proof PVC tube.

Kitchen: first of all, there are many human foods that can be harmful to dogs, therefore, your puppy should be in its crate or playpen or out of your kitchen any time you are preparing food.

Bathroom: bathroom cupboards and drawers or the side of a bathtub where you may leave your shaving supplies can hold many dangers for a young and curious Vallhund.

Kleenex, cotton swabs, Q-tips, toilet paper, razors, pills, and soap left within your puppy's reach are an easy target that could result in an emergency visit to your veterinarian's office.

Family members need to put shampoos, soap, facial products, makeup, and accessories out of reach or safely inside a cabinet or drawer.

Bedroom: if you don't keep your shoes, slippers and clothing safely behind doors, you may find that your puppy has claimed them for their new chew toys. Be vigilant about keeping everything in its safe place, including jewelry, hair ties, bills, coins, and other items small enough for them to swallow in containers or drawers, and secure any exposed cords or wires.

If you have children, make sure they understand that, especially while your puppy is going through its teething stage, that they must keep their rooms picked up and leave nothing that could cause a choking problem to the puppy lying about on the floor or within their reach.

Living Room: we often spend many hours in our cozy gathering places to watch movies or play games, and often the living areas of our homes will have many items that are very enticing for a curious and teething puppy, such as books, magazines, pillows, iPods, TV remotes and more.

You will want to keep your home free of excess clutter and remain vigilant about straightening up and putting things out of sight that could be tempting to your puppy.

Office: we often spend a great deal of time in our home offices, which means that our puppy will want to be there, too, and it will be curious about all the items an office has to offer, including papers, books, magazines, and electrical cords.

Although your puppy might think that rubber bands or paper clips are fun to play with, allowing these items to be within your puppy's reach could end up being a fatal mistake if your puppy swallows them.

Plants: These are also a very tempting target for your puppy's teeth, so you will want to keep them well out their reach. If you have floor plants, they will need to be moved to a shelf or counter or placed behind a closed door until your curious fur friend grows out of the habit of putting everything in its mouth. Also keep in mind that many common houseplants are poisonous to dogs. Be sure to read through the list as many are truly common house and yard plants.

Garage and Yard: there are obvious as well as subtle dangers that could seriously harm or even kill a Swedish Vallhund puppy that are often found in the garage or yard. Some of these might include antifreeze, gasoline, fertilizers, rat and mice poison, snail and slug poison, weed killer, paint, cleaners and solvents, grass seed, bark mulch and various insecticides.

If you are storing any of these toxic substances in your garage or garden shed, make certain that you keep all such bottles, boxes, or containers inside a locked cabinet, or stored on high shelves that your puppy will not be able to reach. Even better, choose not to use toxic chemicals anywhere in your home or yard.

Chapter 17: Bringing Your Vall Home

Breeders will usually let puppies go to their new owners at 8 weeks or shortly after. By then, the puppy is weaned and eating puppy food. The breeder has probably started housetraining the puppy as well.

1. Hypoglycemia Warning

Some breeders suggest adding a little sugar (1 teaspoon per 8 oz) to the puppy's water during its first few days with you. You might check that with your veterinarian. This is to avoid hypoglycemia or low blood sugar.

Hypoglycemia can occur in any puppy, usually only when they're less than 13 weeks old. Stress from air shipping and meeting the new family could trigger it. The puppy may change from an active dog to a weak, shaky, wobbly animal very quickly. Facial tremors are common. If the puppy is alert, feed it honey or corn syrup. If the animal slips into a coma, rub the sugary substance on its gums and take the animal to the veterinarian.

2. Before You Go

Before you go, vacuum your floors and do a last-minute check of every room to make sure that everything that could be a puppy hazard is carefully tucked away out of sight and that nothing is left on the floor or low down on shelves where a curious puppy might get into trouble.

Close most of the doors inside your home, so that there is just one or two rooms that the puppy will have access to. Get out a puppy pee pad and have it ready.

Take either a hard-sided kennel or soft-sided travel bag with you and make sure that it is securely fastened to the seat of your vehicle with the seatbelt system and lined with a puppy pee pad.

3. At the Breeders

If you go to the breeder or shelter and the mother dog is still there, rub a towel or blanket on her to keep with the puppy. If you pick the dog up at the airport, the breeder should have shipped the puppy with a towel with the mother's scent on it.

Even though you will be tempted to hold your new puppy in your lap on the drive home, this is a very dangerous place for her to be in case of an accident. If you have a friend who can drive for you, sit beside your puppy her crate in the back seat.

4. Back Home, Training Begins!

Once home, place the collar and leash on the puppy while in the car. Before going inside, let the puppy stay outside until she at least pees, then go inside.

If your puppy has trouble walking on any of your floors, don't laugh and say how cute. If he stumbles and splays his legs, he could injure his hips. Put a carpet remnant or other material he can walk on for his play times. And keep him away from stairs and jumping opportunities as long as you can.

At home, let the puppy explore the room where she will live and sleep. Let the puppy find its water and food dish. (Some owners have a crate in their bedroom for the puppy to sleep at night.) Then, if you have a playpen, show her to her bed and potty (dog pad in low plastic pan). If you're using a crate, introduce the pup to it. If you're using the crate, you'll have to get up during the night to take the pup outside or shut her in a small room (bathroom) with a potty of some sort.

During the day, stay in the room with the puppy as much as possible. Let the children and other adults come in and out of the room. The dog is a herd animal and needs to meet her pack. If you have cats or other dogs, let them investigate but referee.

Let the puppy sleep as much as she wants. Take her out of her crate or playpen to play for a few minutes every hour or so and take her outside to evacuate on a schedule. Most puppies can hold their urine for one hour plus one hour for every month of age. So for an eight-week-old puppy, take her outside at least every three hours to the area of the yard you want it to use. Also take the puppy outside right after it eats. Praise the dog when she evacuates outside -- this is the place for treats!

Your puppy may have loose stools from all the excitement. Usually this can be stopped by adding a little canned pumpkin to his food – the kind without pie spices.

After your puppy's evening meal, take her outside approximately 20 minutes later to relieve herself.

So far your puppy has only been allowed in only one or two rooms of your home, as you have kept the other doors closed, so keep it this way for the first few days.

Before it's time for bed, again take your puppy outside for a very short walk to the same place where she last relieved itself and make sure she pees before going inside.

Before bed, if the room the puppy will sleep in is not very warm, prepare your puppy's hot water bottle and wrap it in a towel so that it won't be too hot for her.

5. Off to Bed

The first few nights expect the puppy to whine. Try a radio or a ticking clock to comfort her. Also, you could get up once or twice during the night to comfort the pup and take it outside. While it's natural for you to want to take the cute little thing to your bed, it is best for the puppy that she learns where her sleeping place is. It won't take long for your puppy to go happily to bed.

Chapter 18: Your Vall's First Days at Home

During the first week, you and your new puppy will be getting settled into your new routine, which will involve you getting used to your puppy's needs as she also gets used to your usual schedule.

Be as consistent as possible with your waking and sleeping routine, getting up and going to bed at the same time each day, so that it will be easier for your puppy to get into the flow of her new life.

First thing in the morning, take your puppy outside immediately to relieve herself at the place where they last went. You may need to carry her outside and put the collar and leash on a few minutes later.

When you bring her back inside, you can let her follow you so she gets used to their new leash and/or harness arrangement.

When your puppy is not eating or napping, she will want to explore and have little play sessions with you. These times will help you bond with your puppy more and more each day.

You can also start training the puppy -- she won't be able to tell the difference between training and play if you don't do the same thing too many times. Reinforce what it has already learned at the breeder's.

You will also need to make sure that she's eating and drinking enough throughout the day, so set regular feeding times at least three times a day.

Set specific times in the day when you will take your puppy out for a little walk on leash and harness, so that she is not only going outside when she needs to relieve herself, but she is also learning to explore her new neighborhood with you beside her.

Be very careful not to drag your puppy she stops or pulls back on the leash.

When your Vallhund is still very young, you will not want to walk for a long time as she will get tired easily, so keep your walks to no more than 15 or 20 minutes during your first week and if she seems tired or cold, pick her up and carry her home.

Avoid having the puppy jump. She'll look like a tough little lady but remember to coddle those knees and hips. Walking is great, as is running, but remember not to fatigue the poor thing. People who do dog training for sports like agility, usually train them on the courses but don't do any jumps until a dog is well over a year old. And when they start jumping, they lower the height until right before a competition.

Source: commons.wikimedia.org Author : Yitzachmmeyer

Chapter 19: House Training

How long will it take to house train your puppy? It depends. The crate or playpen provides a base for training that confines the dog to a specific area of the house and provides good results. Your goal is to have the dog go six to eight hours before needing to relieve itself.

1. Crate

Many owners now use the crating method:

- It may take as little as two or three weeks if someone is home with the dog day and night and you establish an eating and training schedule and stick to it.

- Place the crate in a room with a floor easily cleaned and where family gathers often. The kitchen is a good location.

- Feed the dog at the same time every day. Don't free feed.

- Take the dog outside to urinate every hour for each month of age, plus after eating, after puppy wakes up, and after puppy's active playing.

- At this time, if you are teaching your pup to ring a doorbell to go outside, let it ring the bell before you go out the door even if you're carrying him.

- When outside use the same words: maybe use "out" or "outside" when you pick the puppy up. And then place the puppy where you want it to urinate and use another word such as "go" or "go go". Wait for five minutes or so. If nothing happens, go back inside and try again in half an hour. If the dog "goes", reward it with both words such as "good go" and a treat.

- Use a crate that is just big enough for the puppy's bed and chew toy. Not large enough for it to "go" in the crate. Make sure the bed is waterproof though; there will be accidents. No food or water in the crate. The crate is the puppy's cave not a jail.

- Let the dog out of the crate for short periods every hour, 10 or 15 minutes to start. These periods can be extended or shortened depending upon the dog's ability to avoid "accidents".

- The dog is locked in the crate at night and during the daytime when no one is there.

- No water dish at night.

- At first, set an alarm once or twice at night to take the dog outside.

2. Playpen

A variation of crating is to use a dog playpen.

- Playpens are large enough for the puppy's bed and a toilet (dog pad and low plastic pan) as well as room to romp a bit.

- Still maintain the schedule above, but this option gives the puppy a chance to "go" if you are away from home or sleep through the night.

- This process takes longer than the crating, as you have to then train the puppy off the puppy pads.

- Playpens allow the puppy to be "in" the room with its family but not underfoot. Still take out for longer and longer times.

3. Other options

If you live in an apartment in the city you may train the puppy to a puppy toilet (the dog pad and plastic pan) as outlined above but this will be your dog's primary way for urination. You will still have the dog "go" outside when possible. There are also dog litter boxes and litter similar to those for cats.

Rather than using a playpen, some owners use a small room with a puppy toilet to confine the puppy. The downside of this is the puppy isn't living so close to the family. Family members are more likely to take the puppy to other areas of the house and experience more "accidents".

4. House Training an Older Dog

If possible, find out what an older dog's habits are before you take it home. Your dog may already respond to a particular word and may walk to the door to indicate it needs to go outside.

- When you bring an adult dog home you need to follow the same process as with a puppy: Be with your dog all day for the first few days.

- Crate or confine the dog to a small area when you can't watch it. Provide a dog pad if you leave it alone for a long time.

- Feed on a regular schedule. Don't let it free feed. (You can put treats in hollow toys for its long alone times).

- Take it outside on a regular schedule.

- If the dog needs to urinate more than you feel it should (again, rule of thumb is one hour for each month of age up to six or seven hours) check with your veterinarian. There may be a medical problem.

Chapter 20: Common Mistakes to Avoid

1. Sleeping in Your Bed

Many of us make the mistake of allowing a crying puppy to sleep in your bed, and while this may help to calm and comfort a new puppy, it will set a dangerous precedent that can result in behavioral problems later in her life. Also, a tiny puppy can easily be crushed by a sleeping human body.

As much as you may hate to hear your puppy crying the first couple of nights in her kennel, a little tough love at the beginning will help her learn to both love and respect you as their leader.

2. Picking Your Vallhund Up at the Wrong Time

Never pick your puppy up if they display fear or growl at an object or person, because this will be rewarding them for unbalanced behavior.

Instead, your puppy needs to be gently corrected by you, with firm and calm energy so that she learns not to react with fear or aggression.

3. Playing Too Hard or Too Long

Many humans play too hard or allow their children to play too long with a young puppy. You need to remember that a young puppy tires very easily and especially during the critical growing phases of their young life, she needs its rest.

4. Hand Play

Always discourage your puppy from chewing or biting your hands, or any part of your body for that matter. If you allow her to do this when a puppy, she will want to continue to do so when she has strong jaws and adult teeth.

Do not get into the habit of playing the "hand" game, where you rough up the puppy and slide them across the floor with your hands, because this will teach your puppy that your hands are playthings.

When your puppy is teething, they will naturally want to chew on everything within reach, and this will include you. As cute as you might think it is, this is not an acceptable behavior and you need to gently, but firmly, discourage the habit.

A light flick with a finger on the end of a puppy nose, combined with a firm "No" when they are trying to bite human fingers will discourage them from this activity.

5. Distraction and Replacement

When your puppy tries to chew on your hand, foot, or your clothing, or anything else that is not fair game, you need to firmly and calmly tell them "No", and then distract them by replacing what they are not supposed to be chewing with their chew toy.

Make sure that you happily praise them every time they choose the toy to chew on.

If the puppy persists in chewing on you, remove yourself from the equation by getting up and walking away. If they are really persistent, put them inside their kennel with a favorite chew toy until they calm down.

Always praise your puppy when they stop inappropriate behavior so that they begin to understand what they can and cannot do.

Chapter 21: Bonding With Your Vallhund

You will begin bonding with your puppy from the very first moment you bring it home from the breeders.

This is the time when your puppy will be the most distraught as she will no longer have the guidance, warmth and comfort of her mother or litter mates, and you will need to take on the role of being your new puppy's center of attention.

Your daily interaction with your puppy during play sessions and especially your disciplined exercises, including going for walks on leash, and teaching commands and tricks, will be the best bonding opportunities.

Do not make the mistake of thinking that "bonding" with your new puppy can only happen if you are playing or cuddling together, because the very best bonding happens when you are kindly teaching rules and boundaries.

Source: commons.wikimedia.org Autho: Erikkson

Chapter 22: Puppy Training from Day One

1. Chief Trainer of Dog and Family

Someone in the family has to be in charge of training. The family trainer is in charge of making sure the Vallhund is being trained but also must make sure the family is trained as well!

You'll have to start by training yourself. Puppy classes, and later obedience or other dog group training may not be able to start until the puppy's vaccinations are complete or nearly so. To get ready for the trainer role, go online and see what other people find most effective. There are many very good videos available online to address every training situation. And don't forget – if your puppy or dog get stuck in a bad habit and you can't fix it – ask for help—from other SV owners on social websites, from trainers, or from your breeder or veterinarian.

2. Vocabulary

Don't confuse your SV by using more than one word for each action. Decide upon what needs to be learned and pick one word for it. Find out from the breeder what words your puppy already knows. Go online and see what other people have found most helpful. Watch dog training videos and get hints from them. Keep a vocabulary list on the fridge listing each word and the action desired.

3. Basic commands

Treat this as playtime, but don't go more than 3-5 minutes at first. Be in a quiet place without distractions. Have the dog's collar and leash on. You should kneel or sit.

4. Using a Clicker

The Vallhund responds well to clicker training. Click the clicker the second the puppy does what you want. Try non-treat rewards at first -- saying 'Good Dog' or giving a belly rub or quick cuddle.

5. Treats and clicker

For beginning a new trick, often a treat is needed. When the dog responds correctly, click the clicker and then immediately give him a treat.

6. Basic Commands

Below are a few basic commands.

- No

This word will come naturally to you. Just try to say it in the same tone as you'd say "come". Use "no" and then deflect the dog's attention with a toy or another object.

- Sit

Your puppy may already know this one. Say "sit" or use the puppy's name and "sit". At the same time hold your hand over his head and push him at the back into sitting position. Say "good dog" and reward him with a belly rub or whatever he likes. Then repeat. And repeat. It won't be long before he'll sit at either the voice command or your hand over his head.

- Down

This command is similar to "sit" but your puppy may be confused about what's expected. You can push his rear down while sliding your arm under his forelegs to take him from the sit to down position. When his belly is on the ground he's down. Click, reward as before.

- Stay

Start with "sit" and then "stay". Later, "down" and "stay". When working on "stay", stand to the right of the dog facing in the same direction. Say "stay" and step forward. If the dog moves with you, ask the dog to "sit", then move forward again. The dog will eventually stay for a few seconds and you'll click and reward. Continue walking further and further away and make the stays longer and longer.

- Come

Reserve your best treats for this one. If your dog doesn't learn to "come" you'll always be at risk of his running away from you into dangerous situations. Have the puppy on a long lead, let him wander to the end of it then say "come". You can wave your arms and act excited to have him come. Click when he comes to you and reward with "Good Dog", a dance, or a treat. When outside, you may need to use a whistle for "come" if your voice is weak.

Do this repeatedly until you can combine "come" and "sit".

Later, you can combine "stay" and "come" into a hide-and-seek game for your puppy in the house. Go further and further away from him before saying "come".

- Touch

The "touch" command starts with your training the dog to touch your hand with his nose. This command is useful as when you say "touch" the dog will come right up to you. It is also a command that you can use later to teach him to learn the words for several toys or to play ball.

7. Vallhund Traits and Training

You may need to damp down some strong Vallhund instincts such as nipping at the heels, overly herding (or herding only the animals you want it to), barking, and shyness or over-reaction to noises.

- Nipping

Earlier I warned you not to "hand play" with your puppy. Similarly, don't let the puppy nip at anybody. If it does nip you, yelp like a puppy, lightly tap its nose, say your word for stop -- "off" and "leave it" are good ones, and give the dog its toy. Stop any play and ignore the dog for a while

Make sure everyone the puppy comes in contact with discourages nipping. Don't let young children correct the dog other than use the family's 'stop' word, provide a toy, and leave the dog alone.

- Overly Herding

If your puppy tries to herd children, use your stop command. Until you are sure of your dog, keep him on a leash.

When your dog has mastered basic commands, has been to puppy training and any other obedience classes it needed, you can begin to train him in games that release energy and take advantage of his innate herding ability. Soccer with another person or dog is a good place to start.

And later, your dog will enjoy playing other games designed for herding dogs, such as Treibball in which dogs compete in herding large exercise balls. (See Chapter 29 for games and sports).

- Barking

Your Swedish Vallhund is a watchdog and will bark. Some say its bark is a little high-pitched and irritating. You can control watchdog barking with training. Settle upon your word for "please be quiet" -- "hush" is a good one. When the puppy barks, clap your hand or make some other sharp sound (some use a can full of coins and drop in near them) and say "hush". Give a "Good Dog" and divert his attention. You don't want him to stop barking at people coming toward your home, just to limit it.

- Other barking:

Your puppy may do 'lonesome' barking in its crate. Covering the crate with a sheet may stop this.

Being sure your puppy is getting plenty of exercise will reduce 'boredom' barking. Make sure he has chew toys and hollow toys with treats to play with when alone. Otherwise, continue with "hush" training.

Don't let the dog stay by itself too long in the yard and get in a 'I just love to bark' habit.

8. Socialization

These puppies need to be socialized to every type of person and animal it will meet during its life. It needs to meet men, women, elderly people, and people in wheelchairs and on crutches, children, dogs, cats, and whatever else will be in your puppy's life. Have strangers hold the dog. Stand out on a busy street and let people stop and meet your puppy. During the first months you cannot do this too often.

9. Habitualization

Just like the many living groups your Vallhund needs to meet, it also needs to be close to cars, trains, and buses, hear horns, bells, machinery, and loud voices while it is still a young puppy. If something frightens your puppy give it space from the cause but don't coddle it. Then go back day after day until your puppy doesn't react. Go for short rides and find new things as often as you possible can.

10. Food Aggression

You don't want your dog to snap or bite if someone tries to take his food dish away. Food aggression is often the only reason that shelter dogs are euthanized. To train your dog not to guard his dish, start by not letting him eat alone. Don't snatch his dish away but be with him while he eats; chat away and pat him. Maybe jiggle his dish. Later, feed him just part of his meal and come and add food to the dish. Make him know that people are only going to do good things during mealtimes.

If your puppy does show food aggression, seek help from a trainer.

11. Puppy Classes

A well-run puppy kindergarten is safe for your puppy. You want a place that disinfects the floor and anything your puppy comes in contact with before every class. The facility will have rules on vaccinations and require proof from every puppy. Check with your vet if you are unsure.

These are great opportunities for your puppy to meet other dogs in a safe environment. (And you to meet other dog owners). Start as soon as your puppy's vaccination schedule allows – 10 weeks is a good time. Don't get too upset if the training method doesn't fit your particular dog. Learn what you can. If possible find a training facility that offers a wide range of training ... advanced obedience, and fun stuff such as agility, tracking and other activities your SV will enjoy.

12. When Can You Let Your SV Off the Leash?

There are two issues here: your dog and the law.

- Your Swedish Vallhund

So much depends upon your community and other dogs. You may have trained your dog to "come" every time, but you could meet other off-lead dogs who attack your dog when she is too far for you to help her. To be safe, have your SV on a leash (long leads give her quite a bit of freedom) unless in a fenced area or in the countryside (that's free of livestock).

- Leash Laws

Most leash laws for non-dangerous dogs are at the local community level. There are some national and state laws concerning letting your dog go loose (unaccompanied and off your premises) and letting your dog off leash in national parks or farmlands where livestock is grazing. (Most of these laws give the farmer the right to shoot your dog).

In the US there are some state laws concerning off leash dogs. New Hampshire forbids dogs off leash on lands where there are game birds or quadrupeds. Massachusetts requires chains or leash for dogs in public rest areas. Michigan requires dogs in heat be on leash when off the owners premises.

UK laws tend to stress only that the dog be under control. There are signs when a leash is required or if no dogs are allowed at all.

Australia, Western Australia and New Zealand's laws are generally dictated by each community. The trend here is for dogs to be required to be on leash in most public places unless they are not allowed at all.

In the US, Michigan State University, College of Law, Animal Legal and Historical Center has individual state dog laws. The Governments of Western Australia has a nice table on their website providing the actual dog laws for each community. In other areas, you'll have to check for your local communities laws.

Chapter 23: Puppy's Dinner Time

1. Avoid Obesity and Bone Problems

There are two things about the Swedish Vallhund and food to remember:

- The SV is prone to obesity.

- The SV grows slowly. It will reach adult size in 16-20 months. If fed too much during this growth period, especially of processed foods fortified with calcium and minerals, the bones will grow too quickly and exacerbate the SV's tendency toward hip and knee problems. The most important factors in preventing these developmental orthopedic conditions are rate of growth (which is driven by calories eaten) and dietary calcium level.

2. First Days

So, as I've said earlier, when you bring your puppy home keep it on the same food it had at the breeder. If the move has led to diarrhea add a bit of canned unseasoned squash to his food.

Make gradual changes. If the breeder's food is dry food, in a few weeks I'd transition slowly to feeding primarily a canned wet food. You'll want to look for a label that has the lowest calcium level and avoid too many grains (including rice) -- it needn't be all protein. The lower calcium puppy foods will probably be labeled puppy food for large breeds.

Some of the things you'll look for on the label are a named animal source of protein; food high in meat protein & natural fats and oils; no byproducts, animal or vegetable; no added chemicals to color, flavor or preserve the food; essential vitamins and minerals. To see what you'll be getting in the can, check a website such as Dog Food Advisor which lists all the brands and will tell you which have unhealthy ingredients.

Feed the puppy three or four times a day until it is at least one year of age. Fifteen minutes should be a good feeding time. Then discard anything left; if you have a slow steady eater, let it eat a little longer. These meals should provide most of your puppy's nutrition.

3. Puppy Treats

One way to avoid overfeeding is to limit the number of doggy treats. Don't reward the puppy with treats if "Good Boy" and "Good Girl" is an effective reward. Showing love and approval to your puppy is often all it needs. Or put something healthy inside a hollow chew toy. Save the treats for training when your pup has trouble concentrating.

Chapter 24: Chewy Things for Pup and Dog

Your Vallhund will always love a good chew. He'll be chewing out of discomfort when teething but out of his love of it the rest of his life.

When he's two or three weeks old he'll start to get his baby teeth. -- the needlelike sharp ones. They'll be all in by the time he's 2 months old. Then when he's around 4 months old his adult teeth will begin to come in. They should all be in by his 8th month or a little longer.

At some point when you are brushing, make sure all the baby teeth are out. Sometimes their roots don't dissolve and need pulling.

1. Chew Toys

A Vall can destroy a fuzzy stuffed toy in minutes. Some say, though, he should be given the chance to do it occasionally. If you agree, go for the canvas squeaky toys, they'll last the longest. But don't let him play with it in private.

He'll eventually tear a rope toy to pieces but these are good for tug-of-war. Play with it then put it away.

Good sturdy toys for your Viking are the black or blue Kong toys. If he doesn't chew them right away, put a touch of peanut butter on the inside. Another sturdy brand are the Zogoflex toys that come in shapes that might entertain him.

When you're around, tennis balls are good. He'll wreck them, but they're cheap. Don't let him destroy them enough to actually fall into pieces he could eat.

2. Chews to avoid:

- Pebbles and small sticks

When a puppy, he may pick up small things from the ground that are either choking hazards or that will do damage to his gut. When you are outside with him, watch for it. If you leave him outside semi-attended, have him in the exercise pen or other enclosure on grass that's been scoured for harmful items.

- Rawhide

Rawhide is soaked in an ash/lye solution to remove every particle of meat, fat and hair and then further soaked in bleach to remove remaining traces of the ash/lye solution. Now that the product is no longer food, it no longer has to comply with food regulations.

While the hide is still wet it's shaped into rawhide chews, and upon drying it shrinks to approximately 1/4 of its original size.

Further, arsenic based products are often used as preservatives, and antibiotics and insecticides are added to kill bacteria that also fight against good bacteria in your dog's intestines.

The collagen fibers in the rawhide make it very tough and long lasting which makes this chew a popular choice for humans to give to their dogs because it satisfies the dog's natural urge to chew while providing many hours of quiet entertainment.

Sadly, when a dog chews a rawhide treat, it ingests many harsh chemicals. Also, when your dog swallows a piece of rawhide, that piece can swell up to four times its size inside your dog's stomach, causing anything from mild to severe gastric blockages that could become life threatening and require surgery.

- Pigs Ears

These treats are actually the ears of pigs, and while most dogs will eagerly devour them, they are extremely high in fat, which can cause stomach upsets, vomiting and diarrhea for many dogs.

Pigs ears are often processed and preserved with unhealthy you will not want to you're your dog. While pig ears are generally not considered to be a healthy treat choice for any dog, they should be especially avoided for your SV who you know is at risk of being overweight.

- Hoof Treats

Many humans give cow, horse and pig hooves to their dogs as treats because they consider them to be "natural".

The truth is that after processing these "treats" they retain little, if any, of their "natural" qualities.

Hoof treats are processed with preservatives, including insecticides, lead, bleach, arsenic-based products, and antibiotics to kill bacteria that can also harm the good bacteria in your dog's intestines. If all bacteria are not killed in these meat-based products before feeding them to your dog, it could also suffer from diseases such as Salmonella poisoning.

Hooves can also cause chipping or breaking of your dog's teeth as well as perforation or blockages in your dog's intestines.

3. Healthy Chews

- Hard Treats

There are so many choices of hard, or crunchy treats available that come in many varieties of shapes, sizes and flavors, that you may have a difficult time choosing. If your puppy or dog will eat them, hard treats will help to keep their teeth cleaner.

Whatever you do choose, read the labels and make sure that the ingredients are high quality and appropriately sized.

- Soft Treats

Soft, chewy treats are also available in a wide variety of flavors, shapes and sizes. These are often used for training purposes as they have a stronger smell.

- Dental Treats

  Dental treats or chews are designed with the specific purpose of helping your dog to maintain healthy teeth and gums. They usually require intensive chewing and are often shaped with high ridges and bumps to exercise the jaw and massage gums while removing plaque build-up near the gum line. As you're going to watch your Vallhund's weight, I'd suggest limiting the dental treats and use toys designed for dental health instead.

- Freeze-Dried and Jerky Treats

Freeze-dried and jerky treats offer a tasty morsel most dogs find irresistible as they are usually made of simple, meaty ingredients, such as liver, poultry and seafood. These treats are usually light and easy to carry around, which means they can also be great as training treats.

- Human Food Treats

You will want to be very careful when feeding human foods to dogs as treats, because many of our foods contain additives and ingredients that could be toxic.

Be certain to choose simple, fresh foods with minimal or no processing, such as lean meat, poultry or seafood.

Yes, we humans love to treat our dogs, whether for helping to teach the new puppy to go pee outside, teaching the adolescent dog new commands, for trick training, for general good behavior, or for no reason at all, other than that they just gave us the "look".

Make sure the treats you choose are high quality, so that you can help to keep your Vallhund both happy and healthy, and generally, the treats you feed should not make up more than approximately 5% of its daily food intake.

Chapter 25: Feeding Your Adult Vallhund Dog

You will slowly change your puppy's diet to adult dog products. Do this gradually as you also change feedings from three to four a day to two.

So, what to buy? (Or make?)

From the beginning, commercially-made dog food has sprung a massively lucrative and the vastly confusing industry has only recently begun to evolve beyond those early days of feeding our dogs the dregs of human leftovers because it was cheap and convenient for us.

Even today, the majority of dog food choices have far more to do with being convenient for us humans to serve than it does with being a diet truly designed to be a well-balanced, healthy food choice for a dog.

The dog food industry is big business and as such, because there are now almost limitless choices, there is much confusion and endless debate when it comes to answering the question, "What is the best food for my dog?"

Educate yourself by talking to experts and reading everything you can find on the subject, plus taking into consideration several relevant factors, will help to answer the dog food question.

For instance, where you live may dictate what sorts of foods you have access to. Other factors to consider will include the particular requirements of your dog, such as their age, energy and activity levels.

Next will be expense, time and quality. While we all want to give our dogs the best food possible, many humans lead very busy lives and cannot, for instance, prepare their own dog food, but still want to feed a high quality diet that fits within their budget.

1. Canine Eating Anatomy

However, perhaps most important when choosing an appropriate diet for our dogs, is learning to be more observant of Mother Nature's design and taking a closer look at a dog's teeth, jaws and digestive tract.

While humans are herbivores who derive energy from eating plants, our canine companions are carnivores, which means they derive their energy and nutrient requirements from eating a diet consisting mainly or exclusively of flesh or animal tissues (i.e. meat).

- Teeth

The first part of your dog you will want to take a good look at when considering what to feed them will be their teeth.

Unlike humans, who are equipped with wide, flat molars for grinding grains, vegetables, and other plant-based materials, canine teeth are all pointed because they are designed to rip, shred and tear into animal meat and bone.

- Jaw

Another obvious consideration when choosing an appropriate food source for your dog, is the fact that every canine is born equipped with powerful jaws and neck muscles for the specific purpose of being able to pull down and tear apart their hunted prey.

The structure of the jaw of every dog is such that it opens widely to hold large pieces of meat and bone, while the mechanics of a dog's jaw permits only vertical (up and down) movement that is designed for crushing.

- Digestive Tract

A dog's digestive tract is short and simple and designed to move their natural choice of food (hide, meat and bone) quickly through their systems.

Most vegetable and plant matter requires more time to break down in the gastrointestinal tract, which in turn, requires a more complex digestive system than the canine body is equipped with.

This is why some whole vegetables look pretty much the same going into your dog as they do coming out the other end.

Given the choice, most dogs would never choose to eat plants or vegetables and fruits over meat, however, we humans continue to feed them a kibble based diet that contains high amounts of vegetables and grains and low amounts of meat.

How much healthier and long lived might our dogs be if, instead of largely ignoring nature's design for our canine companions, we chose to feed them whole, unprocessed, species-appropriate food?

Whatever you decide to feed your SV, keep in mind that, just as too much wheat, other grains and other fillers in our human diet is having detrimental effects on our health, the same can be very true for our dogs.

Our dogs are also suffering from many of the same life threatening diseases that are rampant in our human society as a direct result of consuming a diet high in genetically altered, impure, processed and packaged foods.

2. The Raw Diet

While some of us believe we are killing ourselves as well as our dogs with processed foods, others believe that there are dangers in feeding raw foods.

Those who are raw feeding advocates believe that the ideal diet for their dog is one which would be very similar to what a dog living in the wild would have access to, and these are dog owners often opposed to feeding their dog any sort of commercially manufactured pet foods, because they consider them to be poor substitutes.

On the other hand, those opposed to feeding their dogs a raw or biologically appropriate raw food diet, believe that the risks associated with food-borne illnesses during the handling and feeding of raw meats outweigh the purported benefits.

Interestingly, even though the United States Food and Drug Administration (FDA) states that they do not advocate a raw diet for dogs, they do advise that for those who wish to take this route, following basic hygiene guidelines for handling raw meat can minimize any associated risks.

Further, high pressure pasteurization (HPP), which is high pressure, water based technology for killing bacteria, is USDA-approved for use on organic and natural food products, and is being utilized by many commercial raw pet food manufacturers.

Raw meats purchased at your local grocery store contain a much higher level of bacteria than raw food produced for dogs because the meat purchased for human consumption is meant to be cooked, which will kill any bacteria that might be present.

This means that dog owners feeding their pets a raw food diet can be quite certain that commercially prepared raw foods sold in pet stores will be safer than raw meats purchased in grocery stores.

Many owners of high energy, working breed dogs will agree that their dogs thrive on a raw or BARF (Biologically Appropriate Raw Food) diet and strongly believe that the potential benefits of feeding a raw dog food diet are many, including:

- healthy, shiny coats
- decreased shedding
- fewer allergy problems
- healthier skin
- cleaner teeth
- fresher breath
- higher energy levels
- improved digestion
- smaller stools
- strengthened immune system
- increased mobility in arthritic pets
- general increase or improvement in overall health

All dogs, whether working breed or lap dogs are amazing athletes in their own right, therefore every dog deserves to be fed the best food available.

A raw diet is a direct evolution of what dogs ate before they became our domesticated pets and we turned toward commercially prepared, easy to serve dry dog food that required no special storage or preparation.

The BARF diet is all about feeding our dogs what they are designed to eat by returning them to their evolutionary diet.

3. The Dehydrated Diet

Dehydrated dog food comes in both raw and cooked forms and these foods are usually air dried to reduce moisture to the level where bacterial growths are inhibited.

The appearance of de-hydrated dog food is very similar to dry kibble and the typical feeding methods include adding warm water before serving, which makes this type of diet both healthy for our dogs and convenient for us to serve.

Dehydrated recipes are made from minimally processed fresh whole foods to create a healthy and nutritionally balanced meal that will meet or exceed the dietary requirements for healthy dogs.

Dehydrating removes only the moisture from the fresh ingredients, which usually means that because the food has not already been cooked at a high temperature, more of the overall nutrition is retained.

A de-hydrated diet is a convenient way to feed your dog a nutritious diet because all you have to do is add warm water, and wait five minutes while the food re-hydrates so your Swedish Vallhund can enjoy a warm meal.

4. The Kibble Diet

While many dog owners are starting to take a closer look at food choices they are making for their furry companions, there is no mistaking that the convenience and relative economy of dry dog food kibble, that had its beginnings in the 1940's and continues to be the most popular pet food choice for most dog friendly humans.

Kibble is not the ideal food for a steady diet for your dog. But if you are going to use it, invest some time in finding the product you can afford which is best for your dog. Corn, wheat, and gluten are commonly high on list of kibble ingredients while many dogs are highly allergic to them. Other ingredients allowed in kibble are modified plastics and rat waste. So, as with choosing puppy food, find what you think is the best kibble and then check it out on a website such as Dog Food Advisor.

5. Homemade Dog Food

Many people are now making their dog's food. Often you'll see recipes online and people exclaiming that the dog loves the food. But don't forget, dogs love their kibble too!

In order to provide healthy homemade food you have to do more than avoid the human foods toxic to dogs. You have to create a diet that has the right protein/fat balance for your dog's age and activity and which will provide the 11 amino acids the dog can't manufacture by itself. You'll need to know which of the carbohydrates you're adding to the recipe also contribute fats. You'll need to know which ingredients to avoid which may cause allergies in your Swedish Vallhund. You'll need to know which foods contribute the fiber, vitamins, and minerals your dog needs.

Some dog food companies such as Just Food For Dog have branched into the homemade food market, offering recipes and supplements so that you can duplicate their products at home.

I applaud those who cook their dog's food. I wouldn't do it myself, however, without consulting a veterinary nutritionist to make sure that I was cooking was best for my own dog. If done correctly, it can be a less expensive way to feed your dog very well.

Chapter 26: Human Foods Toxic to Your SV

Your dog, especially in the mouthing puppy months, will be trying to put everything in its mouth. What follows are foods you need to keep away from it always, but be especially careful of your puppy.

1. Prevention Comes First

Your best rule of thumb is to ban giving your Vallhund any human food. This includes any access to food leftovers and trash containers inside and outside the house. Reinforce this with any adult or child who is around your dog.

2. Be a Detective!

One take-away from this: if your dog starts acting funny or vomits or has diarrhea, check the stools or vomit to see if you recognize any of the foods listed below; look through the house and trash for evidence your dog's been into something dangerous.

3. Know Who to Call

As for your human medical emergency phone numbers, have a pet poison center number, your veterinarian's number, and the local animal emergency hospital or clinic's number in your phone or on your wall and in your car.

Poison Help Lines:

US: ASPCA (888-222-1222) May have $65 (40£) consultation fee; also your veterinarian may have access to ASPCA through a partnership program (you may be charged for service).

US and Canada: Pet Poison Helpline (800-213-6680) $35 (20£) credit card charge.

UK: Call your veterinary clinic; they will have access to poison information service.

Australia: Call your veterinary clinic or emergency veterinary hospital; also the "human" poison control service have answers for some pet poison questions (13 11 26).

New Zealand: As for Australia, call your veterinary clinic or emergency hospital. National Poisons Center may help (0800 764 7666).

4. Some Dangerous Human Foods

- Xylitol

Xylitol is an artificial sweetener that is fatal to dogs. It can be in candies or in mouthwash or toothpaste. The chemical has been known to cause hypoglycemia in dogs and to damage a dog's liver. It's sometimes hard to know the dog has eaten xylitol as it may not show toxicity for days.

- Caffeine

Dogs are more sensitive than humans to the stimulant effects of caffeine. The toxic level of caffeine is about 70 mg/lb. of a healthy dog. This is equivalent to drinking one espresso per pound of dog or eating 15 beans per pound of dog. A lesser dose of caffeine can be fatal if the dog's heart is not healthy.

Coffee beans can are also a choking hazard. More dangerous are the chocolate-covered beans which add the poison contained in chocolate.

More dangerous to dogs is caffeine pills. These should be locked away.

- Chocolate

Chocolate can kill your dog. Consider no amount of chocolate "safe".

Chocolate contains theobromine, the chemical which is poisonous to dogs. The darker the chocolate the more theobromine it has in it. Theobromine is a powerful stimulant that the dog's body has difficulty clearing. Small amounts can cause vomiting and diarrhea; larger amounts (2 oz. of baking chocolate can kill a 20 pound dog) cause increase heart rate and blood pressure and cause seizures.

- Grapes and raisins

Grapes and raisins cause kidney failure in dogs. It is not yet known what chemical in the fruit is so toxic. Some dogs don't seem affected while two or three grapes can kill another dog. Small snack size boxes of raisins have been fatal to dogs.

In addition to grapes and raisins by themselves, be careful of leaving out (or offering to the dog) sweets and breads containing large numbers of raisins that could attract your dog.

- Avocados

Some sources say the avocado fruit, pit, bark, and leaves are toxic to dogs. The tree bark, leaves and pit do contain persin, a toxin that affects birds, horses and cattle. But the toxin doesn't affect dogs. The avocado seed or pit is a dangerous choking hazard in dogs and can also cause a gastrointestinal obstruction.

- Garlic and Onions

Garlic and onions (and others in the family: green onions, shallots, etc.) contain allyl propyl disulfide that damage red blood cells in dogs. They can be raw, cooked, or dehydrated and still be toxic.

Affected red blood cells can rupture or lose their ability to carry oxygen effectively; this results in anemia which, if severe, can cause kidney failure. If you plan to feed your dog any human canned food such as soups -- check the label for any fresh or powered garlic, onion, etc.

- Macadamia Nuts

Macadamia nuts are common in candies and chocolates. The mechanism of macadamia nut toxicity is not well understood, but something in the nuts attacks the nervous system. Dogs become feverish, weak and dull and may have problems with moving their hind legs.

5. Other Harmful Foods

Other foods that are harmful to dogs include bread dough, moldy foods and alcohol. A good detailed discussion of these foods including the timing of symptoms can be found on the American

Society for the Prevention of Cruelty to Animals' website. (www.aspca.org)

Chapter 27: Plants Dangerous to Your Vall

You can go online and search for dangerous plants and get a different list every time. A list of the more common ones is below. Not all of these will kill your dog but they can at least make your dog frightfully sick. For puppies, a good rule is no access to houseplants at all and when outside don't let your puppy or dog chew on any plant, hedge, or tree.

1. List of Common Toxic Plants

Aloe

Amaryllis

Asparagus Fern

Autumn crocus (esp. bulb)

Azaleas (Rhododendron)

Begonia

Caladium

Carnation

Castor beans

Christmas tree pine needles

Chrysanthemum

Coleus

Cyclamen

Daffodils (esp. bulb)

Dieffenbachia

Easter Lilly

Eggplant plant

Elephant ears

English ivy

English Yew

Foxglove

Hops

Hydrangea

Japanese Yew

Jasmine

Jessimine

Jimson weed

Kalanchoe (Mother-in-Law plant)

Lilies

Lily of the Valley

Mistletoe

Morning glory

Nightshade

Oleander

Poinsettia

Potato plant

Rhubarb leaves

Sago palm

Skunk cabbage

Tomato plant

Tulips (esp. bulb)

Water hemlock

The ASPCA has a more complete list of plants toxic to dogs. Also helpful is their list of plants that are not toxic.

2. Eating Grass

Many dogs eat grass. Many wolves and other wild canines also eat grass. Theories have come and gone to explain why and most have been debunked. Most grass-eating dogs do not have a digestive problem they want to relieve by vomiting and most of the dogs eating grass have diets plenty high in fiber. We're left with a dog who could be bored, hungry, or simply likes the taste of grass.

So what's the problem? One problem is the pesticides, herbicides, and fertilizer found on many of today's lawns. Another problem is that plants toxic to dogs could be hiding in the grass.

What's the solution? Keep the chemicals and toxic plants out of your own lawn. If your dog is an avid grass eater, keep an indoor pot of sweat oats (cat grass) for it. And cook up some green beans and mix in with its food. To be on the safe side, check that you're not underfeeding your dog and that you're supplying enough fiber.

Chapter 28: Leaving Home

From the first day your puppy or dog is home, you'll be taking him to see as much of your world as possible – as long as it's safe. Remember that until your puppy has been adequately vaccinated to stay away from other dogs unless you are sure they've also been vaccinated.

1. Visit to the Veterinarian

If you purchased your puppy from a breeder you'll be taking him to the veterinarian within three days or so. This is a health check that makes sense but is also probably required by your contract with the breeder to verify you've received a healthy dog. This first visit will give you a chance to schedule the puppy's needed vaccinations and talk with her about any new questions you may have about caring for your Vall. In these first weeks avoid having the puppy walk on the floor of the office or in the parking lot – he can pick up more than gum!

If the puppy is from a shelter you could delay this first visit a bit as long as the shelter has given you advice about the timing of your puppy's vaccinations. You do want to visit fairly soon just to be an established "patient" in case of a health problem.

It might be a good idea to have a notebook with you every time you visit or call the veterinarian to take notes. It's so easy to forget. Also, bring some treats just in case your puppy is nervous.

2. Meet more people

Continue with socialization and habitualization as described in Chapters 12 and 22, especially during the first few months. This reduces your chances of having a shy, nervous, skittish Vallhund.

3. Leash Training

You've seen them: men and women being pulled down the sidewalk by their dogs looking as if their arms are being pulled out of the socket. Your goal in leash training is to avoid having this happen to you. You want to walk at your pace with your Vall at your side or a bit behind with the two of you connected by a slack leash. No tugging, no pulling.

All it takes is patience and determination – not a miracle. Remember to keep these early training periods short – three minutes or so at a time.

First, the collar. If your puppy is already wearing a collar, fine. If he's not, introduce it slowly and as if it were no big deal. Put it on as he begins to feed. If he tries to take it off, ignore him. Once he stops his antics, take the collar off. Do this several times a day until he wears his collar whenever he's out of his crate. (A small nylon collar is fine).

Second, the leash. A six foot thin nylon leash would be fine. Take it out as part of a game. Show it to him. If he's not afraid of it, clip it to his collar and leave it on as long as you can supervise. (It could get caught on something.) As part of your play, call to him and see if he'll walk with you around the room, entice him with your "good dog". He'll be dragging the leash.

Third, pick up the leash. When he's used to the leash, pick it up. Practice inside. Ask him to sit. Then use your "go" word – "Let's Go" or "Heel" – and when he walks beside you, praise him. Take a few steps and ask him to sit. Praise him. Then, "go" again. Now, the minute he charges ahead and pulls at the leash, stop. Don't pull him back. Call him back. When he comes, praise him. Ask him to sit. Then go. Then sit. Then go. And stop each time he pulls the leash. As long as you never pull the leash and he can't walk if he pulls on the leash, he'll learn at some point that a limp leash is what he wants.

If you have any trouble with this, don't give up. Go online and watch videos to see if there is something you're missing. Also, this will be part of the puppy class and later obedience classes. Whatever you do, don't give up.

You may have your dog under control but be wary of other dogs. If a dog being walked wants to come right up to face your puppy, step in front of your dog, hold up your hand (in a traffic "stop" position), and explain to the dog's walker that your dog is in training.

4. Puppy Classes and Beyond

Find a place that offers a wide range of training, your dog's "club". If there is an organization you can join which gives reduced rates for training and provides a logical series of training from basic obedience to competitive "sports", I would recommend that you join. You can get in the habit of once-weekly training sessions which will keep your Vallhund's active brain engaged. There will also be sports that he can train for as he gets older. Even if some sports, such as animal herding or Treibball may not be offered, being part of such an organization will give you access to many dog people who will know what's available in the area. Often these organizations have reasonable annual fees of $100 (60£) or less; have practice fields for training, and classes for $20-30 (12-18£) a week.

Look for an organization licensed by the American Kennel Club (AKC) and United States Dog Agility Association, Inc. (USDAA) or equivalent.

Start puppy training there if they offer it. Some won't because some multi-use facilities are difficult to clean for the puppy classes.

A good sequence of once-a-week classes would be six weeks of basic puppy obedience and another four to six weeks of more advanced obedience.

Then if rally training is available, take it. This puts your obedience training to work. There are courses with maybe 10 or 15 stations; at each one you'll call or show a different command and your pup will obey. The course is timed so you can track your improvement.

Another helpful course is one that makes sure that you have a reliable "come" command.

Once you have mastered the basics you can go on to have more fun with your SV. Remember, your Vallhund can be a crafty, stubborn dog – don't let him sweet talk you from setting the goals for his behavior.

5. Vehicle Safety

Accidents happen. You don't want your dog loose in the car to fly through the windshield or harm you or your children. Even experienced dog handlers have learned this lesson the hard way.

Continue with the safe transport of your dog you used when you took him home. Use a sturdy crate safely attached to the rear seat when he's a puppy. (Using just the car's safety belt isn't enough. There are crate straps available. Strap the crate so the long side of the crate is against the seat back.) Later, when he's older, you can use a safety harness in the back seat or continue with his crate. It might be cute to watch dogs hanging their heads out the window, but your dog's eyes can be seriously injured doing this.

If the dog is to ride in a truck bed also have it crated or harnessed. It's unsafe, plus several US states and Australia and New Zealand make it illegal to transport unrestrained dogs in truck beds or other open vehicles. Some US states don't allow dogs to sit in the driver's lap. Similarly, in the UK dogs are to be transported such that they don't distract the driver; the law suggests methods of restraint, which have been interpreted as guidelines and not law.

On longer day trips, let your Vallhund out for regular breaks – potty and exercise. Bring a water jug and a bowl if they won't be available. Bring a low volume high protein snack for lunch. Before you know how your dog will do, don't feed him much before you travel any distance.

If you're staying overnight at a friend or relative's house make sure they know the dog is coming and that you bring everything your dog needs with you.

If you're planning to stay at hotels/motels do some research. There are several online services to discover the dog policies of hotels/motels at your destination. Some require deposits and/or surcharges to have your dog stay in the room with you. Some don't allow non-service dogs at all.

6. City Dogs & Public Transportation

If you live in a city, each one will have a different policy for allowing dogs on subways, surface trains and buses. Some require the pet be in a "box" and dog owners have found that covered dog strollers are often accepted. Bigger cities and the UK are probably the most accepting of dogs. In the UK dogs are allowed on trains and buses (at the decision of the driver or personnel) but not the London underground. In Sydney, dogs are allowed on buses if restrained in a "box, basket, or other container"; non-service dogs are not allowed on the trains/subways.

7. Travelling

In the US, your choice is limited for making long trips is to fly or drive. And flying is not possible for most dogs during hot and cold months. Most long-distance human options such as Greyhound and Amtrak do not allow non-service dogs. In Canada, VIA Rail Canada allows non-service dogs to be shipped as checked baggage for a fee if they are in a crate they can stand in. UK allows dogs on the trains and buses at the discretion of driver and train personnel. In New Zealand and Australia most buses and trains do not allow non-service dogs.

If you are flying, double check the airline's policy for allowing dogs. They will have separate rules for taking your dog as carry-on luggage, as checked baggage, and as cargo (cargo = you're not on the same plane). Also, they won't accept dogs when the ground weather is either too hot or too cold – often above 85 °F or below 10 °F.

To take a dog as carry-on luggage he and his carrier have to fit under the seat. This limits the size of a dog to about 15 lbs. (6.8 kg) or one who fits comfortably in a medium Sherpa bag. The federal rules say that dogs need to be at least 8 weeks old but some airlines will insist he be 10 weeks old or older. There will be a fee for this and it still counts as your carry-on piece. The dog has to stay in the carrier in the boarding areas and while in the plane. Airlines differ, but most limit the number of carry-on pets for each flight and require 48-hour notice of your intent. If you go over state lines you'll need proof of vaccination and a health okay from your vet made within 60 days.

Your larger dog needs to be shipped in a crate as checked baggage. Airlines will differ in required crate construction, handles, having wheels or not, number of ventilated sides, etc. You need to make a 48 hour notice and, if you don't have the type of carrier they require, you may be able to buy directly from the airline. There is usually a fixed fee for this and it will count toward any baggage restrictions on your ticket. If you're travelling on more than one airline you'll need to research both. The age and health documents are the same as for a carry-on dog.

Dogs shipped cargo have to meet the same rules as for checked baggage dogs except the health okay from the veterinarian has written within ten days of shipping. Shipping rates vary and may be based upon weight.

The cargo area where dogs travel are lit and temperature controlled. But mistakes do happen. Dogs are taken off at the wrong airport and other mishaps.

8. Specialty Travel Services

There are pet airlines and pet ground services that don't take owners but which have the dogs in the plane cabin or in buses or other vehicles. These services would be available year round but may not be available to all locations. Worth looking into.

There is at least one service, Dog Travel Company, which arranges train and air travel for people who want to, and can afford to, travel with their dogs. (Sample charges from NYC to Miami by sleeper train or aircraft were about $1,400 (845£) one way). No crates, no baggage compartments. They fly executive jets and larger planes for groups. The company also makes dog-friendly cruise, vacation, and hotel reservations.

9. Leaving Dog at Home While You Travel

Sometimes it's better to travel without your Vallhund. If no one will be at home to care for her you have many options: a friend or neighbor; a service which cares for your dog at your home;

boarding your dog at another person's home; or a boarding kennel.

It's a lot to ask of a friend or neighbor; you are lucky if you have one who can look in on your Vall for feeding, sufficient exercise, and companionship. If you are really lucky, they'd stay at your house. Your friend or neighbor probably already knows your dog, which is a plus. A lot depends on your dog and how used she is to being alone. Be careful to block off much of the house so she won't decide to destroy it and buy her some new toys.

You can hire individuals to come walk and feed your dog once or twice a day. Charges for this service will vary by community, but seem to run $15-$30 (9-18£) a visit.

Boarding Kennels exist within a wide range of accommodations, from confinement in a wire cage with perhaps a walk once a day inside the building to pet hotels which offer services comparable to human vacation spots, with off-leash play, swimming and so on. Per day costs can range from $15-$110 (9-66£) a day or more. Just like hotels and motels, there are add-ons at some facilities and not at others so you need to ask for the full menu of potential added costs. Some require their veterinarian to examine the dog and charge for that. Some add on extra meal charges if your dog eats more than once a day. Others charge each time they walk your dog or give him human play time.

One of the least expensive choices these days is offered by people who provide dog care in their own homes. They may do this independently or link to an organization such as Dogvacay. They often have dogs of their own. What they offer is a home life and twenty-four-hour a day supervision and companionship for your dog. They advertise online and you can go visit before choosing the home for your dog. Prices average around $40 (24£) a day and range from $15-$100 (9-60£).

Each community will have different options. Ask your veterinarian and people at your dog "club" for recommendations. Do some research, make calls, then pay some visits. What are you looking for? Do they have strict policies for vaccinations, including kennel cough. Available veterinary services, cleanliness, space for your dog to sleep on raised bed, windows, trained staff with good rapport with dogs, happiness of dogs you see there. How do they provide exercise – large fenced area with off-leash play; leashed walks; private runs, etc.?

When you think you've found what you want, it would be ideal if you could try it for a weekend or two before launching into a longer business trip or vacation. Or just send your Vall for day care a few times.

10. Dog Parks

An off-leash dog park is a large fenced area for your dog to run at will, sniff and laze, and meet and play with other dogs. It may be part of a larger park where dogs are welcome on-leash. There will be good dog parks and not-so-good ones. Many owners won't take their dogs to off-leash parks because of exposure to infection, danger from vicious dogs, and not wanting to risk conflicts with other owners.

- Finding a Dog Park

Talk with your puppy trainer and your vet about the better dog parks in your area. Then visit a few at several different times of the day. At a minimum, you'll want a gated fenced area. Water and waste disposal are usually available. It would be wonderful if the park had separate sections for large and small dogs.

Watch the dogs and their owners. Do the dogs run in packs and play rough? How to they react when a new dog enters the park? Do their owners watch the dogs or just gather for a gab? Is there enough space for your dog to run off by himself or does it get crowded? Are people picking up after their dogs? If you see a real dogfight, how do the owners handle it?

Chat with the other dog owners – what do they do if there's a dogfight? Do you need to carry anything – a walking stick or pepper spray – to stop fights? Are there owners who start arguments – and what time do they usually come?

- The First Visit

Your pup should be at least older than four months old, have all his shots, and you've checked with your veterinarian that it's okay. She'll know if there's an infection going around you should be wary of. There is always a risk of injury or infection at the dog park.

Do not take your dog to an off-leash dog park until he always comes when you call. Practice outside the fence with him on a long lead, or a long rope, until he always comes.

When you've found the best park, go when it's not crowded. Assume all the dogs inside the park know each other. When a new dog enters, they may all approach and sniff and scare your dog. Instead of entering right away, linger outside and let the dogs come to the fence to investigate. Some will get bored and wander off. Then introduce your Vall to the park. Keep him attached to his leash but let it drop when you enter. It'll be easier to rescue him this first time if you need to. Dogs can become aggressive (probably from fear) if they are leashed and they are approached by a dog running free. You can bring treats or a toy but don't offer him any if other dogs are close by. Keep the first visit short, no more than thirty minutes.

If you are the new owner of an adult dog, he may not be as social as most younger dogs. Follow his lead – if he's not interested, or seems aggressive (tight straight body), leave. He may prefer to walk alone with you. Or go really early in the morning and try playing fetch or Frisbee, before any other dogs are there.

- Other Visits

If your Vall likes the park and perks up when you go for the second time, great. But don't force it. When you are there, concentrate on your dog. Always keep your eye on him even if talking with other owners.

Clean up after him. Don't be concerned if he's not playing with other dogs. It's his playtime. If he just wants to sniff the ground for an hour, fine.

Watch him with other dogs for signs that he or his playmates are becoming aggressive. If one puts his muzzle across your dog's shoulder (called T-ing) – time to go. Also, too much stiff body language or real barks and snarls – time to go. Or at least time for him to return to you and calm down.

If your Vall is happy at the park, go as often as you can. If he's not happy, try another. If he doesn't like the next one, try again in a month or so. It may be that he's happier at the dog "club" and the training events there. Whatever you do, make sure he's happy when he's doing it – you know your Vallhund's smile.

Chapter 29: Game & Sports for Your Vallhund

1. Games to Play Inside

Many of the games you can play inside are the building blocks for obedience and sports, others are just fun for you and your family.

Hide and seek. I mentioned this game in the early puppy training. This is built upon a good "sit" or "down" followed by a good "stay". Then you go somewhere else in the house, and test your dog's response to "come". When he does come, celebrate.

Shell game. This begins the basis of scent training and also a good start with the "touch" command. Start with one can and a smelly treat. Let the dog see you put the treat under can. Move it around on the floor. Ask him to "find" and "touch" the can. When he touches the can, lift it and he gets the treat. Then go to two cans, one with and one without a treat. Move them around so he can't tell where the treat is, then go with "find" and "touch" again. When he's good at two cans, move up to three.

Find the "＿". Your Vallhund is a smart dog. Some say he can learn up to 100 words. So don't be afraid of teaching him too many! In this game you wave a toy until he wants it. Get a "sit" and "stay". Hide the toy (at first in plain sight) and ask him to "find Bozo". When he gets the idea, start hiding the toy. When he can find the item in the room, hide it further away.

Fetch. When he's very young you can practice a quiet game of fetch. Clear the area of anything breakable. Ask him to "fetch", "come", and "drop it".

Tug of War. Have one toy he can play this with. A good rope toy or something else that long enough so his teeth won't grip your hand. Give him the toy. Practice "drop it". When he's good at that, then play tug for a while. Don't let him get crazy. So tug, then "drop it". When game's over put the toy away.

Pure fun – many dogs love to play with bubbles – the soap solution and a circular wand toy for children. So sit and blow them.

And parlor tricks. Teach him to crawl, shake hands, roll himself in a blanket – watch videos – whatever other dogs can do, your Vallhund can do also

2. Games to Play Outside

Don't play too long, but give your dog some fun with you in addition to his walks.

Fetch. Bring your inside "fetch" game outside.

Catch. Use a soft toy and toss lightly in an arc toward him saying "catch" at the same time. Praise when he catches; you retrieve the toy when he misses. Move further and further away practicing "catch", "come", and "drop it". When he's good at this it's time for a soft dog Frisbee game. Hint: some dogs will not "drop it" at first – so have two toys and start with a new "catch" just after you ask him to "drop it".

Scent. Drag a treat he really likes over the grass with your dog confined. Have him find it.

Soccer. Use a large ball inflated enough so he can't bite it easily. Just play as if you were teaching a kid.

Start agility. Get him used to walking through a hoop without raising it, run through gates with the jumps.

You can start him swimming in summer or chasing after a stream of water from the hose.

Maze. I saw this in a video. A family dug a maze in the snow in their yard. They had two dogs who were out there playing tag. I imagine that with one dog and a ball or toy you could have fun with this.

Dog beach. If you're lucky you live somewhere you can take your dog to the beach or lake. Most Vallhunds love the water and it's good exercise. Once he's a good swimmer, fetch is good. Be sure to dry his ears afterward.

3. Organized Competitions

a. Confirmation Competitions (Dog Show)

Confirmation shows are those you see on television. In these shows, dogs are evaluated against the standards of their particular breed. Dogs may not participate if they are spayed or neutered, as the purpose of the shows is to evaluate breeding stock. Dogs accumulate points until they reach Champion status. Then they can go on to try to be best of breed in their country, or best dog, etc.

Generally, you would already have an interest in showing dogs before you got your Vallhund. If you had purchased your pup as a pet, you would usually have to spay or neuter him. Also your breeder may co-own your dog and have some say in whether you could show your dog yourself or if you would need a handler.

If you could show the Vall yourself there are rather inexpensive classes in how to pose your dog and show off its gait. Low estimates of gaining Champion status (called finishing) are that it would cost $3,000-$5,000 (1810-3020£) to attend enough shows. This is without a handler. The costs are for transportation and hotels. Most shows are for three days. Entry fees average $30 (18£). Expenses Vallhund owners won't have are for fancy grooming: Valls need the hair around their foot pads trimmed, but otherwise are shown with their natural coat.

People who like showing dogs, love it. They love the travel, meeting other dogs and owners, and the competitions. And their dogs do too.

b. Rally Obedience

In rally competitions, owners and dogs follow a course of several signs telling them what to do. They will teach this at your dog's "club" and it's a good way to practice commands.

In AKC competitions there are three levels. In novice, the dog may be on leash and the owner may use voice and/or hand signals and clapping legs and visit 10-15 stations. Advanced competitors are off leash and visit 12-17 stations. Excellent competitors are off leash, may only use voice commands, and visit 15-20 stations.

There are formal competitions if you wish, leading to title of Rally Advanced Excellent.

c. Obedience Trials

The judging for obedience trials is more demanding than for rally obedience. As for rally obedience, you graduate through three levels:

Novice: You take your dog through some basic obedience commands with and without leash: heel, come, stay sit and stay down.

Open: All commands are performed off leash. Similar to novice but adds retrieval and jumping.

Utility: This level is more complicated. The trial allows hand signals only and includes scent discrimination, directional retrieval (dog follows your hand signal to retrieve a glove) and directed jumping (dog runs away from you; turns and sits; then jumps over hurdle you signaled).

In scent retrieval, you rub your scent on a leather and a metal dumbbell. Your dog needs to pick the dumbbell with your scent from four others.

You can train for these trials as games for your dog or participate in formal trials. In the AKC trials, points lead to Obedience Trial Champion and the organization awards a National Obedience Champion to one dog each year.

d. Agility

Valls love agility! In agility competitions, dogs are timed as they race around a course of several obstacles. For each competition the judge designs the course so not all will be the same. At the Kennel Club (UK) trial the obstacles remind me of the horse show jumping – with wishing wells and water jumps. The AKC in the US has a solid wall jump without the roof of the wishing well and no water jump. The UK Kennel Club also allows judges to have brushes below the jump bars to obscure the landing site – and the water jump has one of these.

Dogs are measured and there are three classes depending upon size. The UK Club advises not training until your dog is a year old and their competitions are open only to dogs 18 months and older. The AKC allows dogs of 15 months and older to compete.

Just to give you an idea of the obstacles so you can mimic some in smaller sizes to play with your pup, I've listed the obstacles used at the UK Kennel Club:

- Single and double hurdles, with or without brush below
- Rising spread jump – jump over two bars at a distance apart and the second one higher
- Long jump – structures like benches but slanting toward the dog are placed a few inches apart and increase in height in increasing heights.
- Tyre – suspended and dogs jump through it
- Table and pause – dogs jump onto the table and must hold for a certain time period
- Wishing well – a solid wall with a roof
- Collapsible tunnel – dog runs into a rigid round entrance and pushes through non-rigid material
- Pipe tunnel – tunnel entirely rigid, usually angled
- A frame – dog runs up and down an A-frame (point at top, no place to stand) with non-slip surface and slats for footing.
- See-Saw – dog runs up the down side and rides the other side to the ground
- Dog Walk – dog runs up narrow slanted plank, across a horizontal one, and down the other side

Your Vall will like this; it's good exercise for you; and your dog "club" will have lessons and competitions. But remember, no jumping until he's at least a year old.

e. Tracking

Tracking is the dog's role in search and rescue. Dogs track human scent trails. In competitions, there are skill levels based upon how long the scent is left before the dog begins, the length of the course, and the terrain it covers.

The AKC, for example, gives TD (for tracking dog) for successful tracking for 440 to 500 yards on a trail ½ to 2 hours old with up to 5 changes of direction. Their TDX (for tracking dog excellent) is over 800 to 1000 yards, the trail is 3 to 5 hours old, and there may be 5 to 7 changes. Their VSD (variable surface dog) is over urban or wilderness trails 3 to 5 hours hold.

Training can begin at your dog's "club". Some trainers use trails aided by treats. Some other trainers believe you should always use humans with a human at the end of the trail to appropriately train your dog.

When you are tracking your dog will wear a harness.

f. Herding
If you live on or near a farm and have free access to a goat, sheep, or cattle herd it makes sense to want to try your Vall at herding.

Even if you have none of the above but are fascinated by the idea, you can still pursue it in some locations. There are herding clubs and herding training businesses which can give you access to livestock ... for a price.

While the Vallhund is a herding dog, as the breed has become several generations older, not all dogs have a herding instinct. Your dog may not be interested. Or he may not be interested when he's a year old but all of a sudden comes alive at three.

There are tests for this instinct given to your dog when he's about a year old. The dog doesn't have to have been trained for herding but must respond well to your "down", "stay", and "come" commands. Usually the tester handles your dog and watches as he meets the herd – which can range from three sheep to a whole flock. The tester protects the sheep from the dog's teeth and watches mostly for your dog's interest in the sheep and his ability to follow basic commands.

Not everyone believes this instinct test is helpful and recommends you first put your dog near livestock a few times a week for a while and then take herding lessons. In the US, lessons seem to range from $25-$50 (15-30£) for a half hour. (Herding will tire your dog quickly).

You may have trouble finding a Vallhund herding trainer but it would be preferable to have one who's had experience with the breed. Often training is given once a week for ten weeks and you can often hire a flock to practice with later. There are also two- and three-day clinics for $200-$300 (120-180£).

Your dog will be trained on sheep who know dogs and are fairly easily moved about. In competitions it's like bull-riding – higher skill levels use sheep much more difficult to handle.

Many dog owners aren't interested in competitions. Getting out into the country and having your dog wheel a herd around and come home tired and happy is enough.

g. Treibball

Treibball takes advantage of your dog's herding instinct. Large exercise balls are edged by the dog's nose or shoulder (no feet) into a goal. In competitions, there are two dogs competing to herd their four balls into the goal first. The dogs must choose only their balls (red or blue). It's fun to watch and the dogs seem to enjoy it.

Your dog doesn't have to compete in formal games. You can set up a goal in your yard and train him to nose the ball and move it into a space or between two "goalposts".

h. Barn Hunt

Barn hunt is a sport for vermin-hunting dogs similar to earthdog for terriers and Dachshunds. Any dog may play if he can enter a tunnel 18" wide and 22" high. The dog participates without a collar and must be over 6 months old.

A course is set up using bales of hay or straw. It includes some climbing challenges and short tunnels. The owner can see the dog all the time and can encourage him. Rats in plastic tubes are hidden and the owner has to signal when he thinks his dog is signing a find. There are fun hunts and formal trials. There are scales of difficulty – different heights of the bales and number of rats and empty traps. Barn Hunt Association, LLC (BHA) runs these competitions. To compete in trials (but not fun hunts) your dog needs to get a one-time BHA registration for $26 (16£) and pay entry fees for the trial. The AKC will add BHA titles to a dog's pedigree.

Chapter 30: Breeding Your Swedish Vallhund

1. Male Dogs

- Sexual development

Your male Vallhund will try mounting as a puppy but then he'll probably stop until he reaches puberty. He'll begin producing sperm at 6-10 months of age. Many young dogs, while they produce sperm, do not produce quality sperm with ability to penetrate eggs. Most breeders wait until the dog has reached physical maturity before breeding him. The peak stud years are between 18 months and five years, with individual variations. If your dog is not neutered, he will remain fertile and sexually active for most of his life.

- The sex act

Dogs (and wolves) have an unusual penis, which has a bulbus glandis at its base. During mating, this swells and causes the penis to be locked inside the bitch aided by contraction of circular muscles of the female's vagina. The two dogs are linked together in what is called a "tie" for several minutes – the average tie is 15-20 minutes but can range from 3-30 minutes. When the tie is established, the dog usually dismounts and positions himself butt to butt with the female. Sometimes the dogs need to be calmed – especially if a larger female starts tossing the male around.

- Why breed your dog?

Given the world's overpopulation of dogs, the only reason you should breed your dog is that he has qualities which would improve the breed in some real way. These could be his positive physical qualities, an absence of recessive genes, a supreme temperament, or incredible talents harking back to the original cattle dogs.

- But don't kid yourself

If you think your dog has the best body, go to a national dog show and show your dog with the champions. If you think he's the best herder, have him compete with other dogs. And so forth. If your dog becomes a champion show dog or wins national working titles, then think of breeding him.

If you do have a dog who would be a valuable stud, don't over breed him. There is some evidence that the high rate of cancers of Golden Retrievers can be traced back the breed's original dog. That dog died of hemangiosarcoma after siring over 1,000 pups. Subsequent breeding of these dogs has made this condition almost impossible for breeders to avoid. Genetic mutations occur all the time; limiting the breeding of a single dog or a single line of dogs can prevent this happening to the Valls.

- Contract with your breeder

If you've purchased your puppy as a pet from a breeder, you will probably have agreed to have him neutered. In many instances, the breeder will be registered as co-owner of your dog until the procedure is done. The breeder can thus block registration of any of your dog's puppies.

If you've purchased your dog with the intent to breed, the breeder may co-own your dog and has interest in the female dogs (bitches) your dog may mate with. This will help you in figuring out the genetics for five generations between your dog and any proposed bitch to make the best match.

- Do you know what's entailed?

Your dog will need proof of excellent health with up-to-date vaccinations and absence of brucellosis; certified hips and knees; and a recent eye exam. You'll need to house the female dog for a week or more away from any other dogs.

Have you assisted in breeding? Do you know what to do if the dogs aren't interested? The bitch may arrive in estrous but not ready for mating. Can you tell when she's ready? What if the tie lasts too long – do you know how to prevent your dog's being damaged?

And the paperwork. You may charge a stud fee or ask for one or more of the puppies or – or both. You'll have a contract drawn up between you and the owner of the female dog. These contracts often specify what health data are needed for both dogs; the number of times the dog will attempt to service the bitch; what will happen if service fails – i.e. if artificial insemination will be performed by a veterinarian; any consideration of a second stud service if the first litter is of one puppy; how the puppies will be sold – with limited registration and spay/neuter contracts; how puppies will not be sold to commercial outlet; and that no puppies will be given to shelters or rescue organizations.

- Accidental or Free-Range Breeding

Do not allow an intact dog come in contact with dogs in season unless for a prearranged breeding for the purpose of maintaining and improving the Swedish Vallhund breed. Professional breeders have facilities to prevent accidental breeding.

2. Female Dogs

- Sexual Development

Your Vallhund bitch will probably have her first season or heat when she's between six months and a year old. It's important she not be bred at this age – it's not good for her health and she won't make the best mother for the puppies. Then as long as she isn't spayed she'll usually go into heat every six months, although some Swedish Vallhunds just go in season once a year.

During first part of her season, proestrus, she'll attract males, have a bloody vaginal discharge, and her vulva will swell. This lasts about nine days during which she will not allow a dog to breed with her. During the following nine days, estrus, she will accept the male. Ovulation occurs two days or so into estrus.

- The sex act; See Male Dogs above.

- Breeding.

When breeding a dog on purpose, the bitch is left with the dog for two or three matings scheduled every other day beginning on 10-14 days after proestrus begins.

Breeders usually wait until the second or third season to begin breeding their female dogs. Depending upon where you'd wish to register the puppies, you'll need to follow guidelines for ages of the bitch and dog; number of litters per bitch; and breeding within a direct family.

The guidelines of the Swedish Vallhund Club of America (SVCA) calls for breeding only bitches at 18 months or older. The SVCA's guidelines call for breeding only two of every three cycles. The UK has a law that requires bitches to be at least 12 months old, and limits litters to one every 12 months and not to exceed six litters. The UK Kennel Club limits the number of litters per bitch to four. The AKC will register puppies from a bitch mated at 8 months and has no guidelines regarding the number of litters during a bitch's lifetime. The Swedish Kennel Club restricts each bitch to five litters.

Some of the registering bodies also restrict mother/son; brother/sister; and father/daughter breeding except under special circumstances.

- What's entailed in breeding your bitch?

As for the male dogs above, your contract with the breeder may prevent you from registering any puppies from a bitch sold as a pet. Also, spay/neuter laws in your community may prevent you from breeding your Vallhund unless you are a licensed professional breeder.

Professional breeders know and love their Vallhunds. To become one of them entails enormous investments in time, money, and emotion. Please see Chapter 11 to see what breeders provide to new dog owners.

You'll need to research genetic issues of the SV breed and of your bitch and determine what characteristics of the male dog will complement her makeup.

Research breeders' ethics of the community you are in; know what's expected of you.

You are responsible for raising a healthy bitch. As in the male dog section above, you will need registration data for three to five generations of your dog's family.

Your dog will need certification of hip and knee health and recent eye examination to rule out genetic abnormality.

Your dog needs to be seen by a veterinarian before breeding; have up-to-date vaccinations and proof of being free of brucellosis (which causes fetal deaths).

You will be responsible for transporting your bitch to the stud dog and staying with her. The bitch goes to the dog as she'll be less dominant there. And she may need to hear your voice. (You can have your dog inseminated by your veterinarian with frozen sperm).

You will have to pay for stud service, with money, puppies or both.

You will pay for the veterinary care of your bitch and the puppies, including vaccinations and genetic testing.

You will pay for feeding the puppies. They will start eating at three weeks and you wouldn't let them go until they are at least eight weeks old.

You will provide the care, cleaning, training, and socialization of the puppies.

You'll have the heartache if any of your puppies are born dead or deformed.

And you will be responsible for the puppies forever, rehoming them as often as needed.

- Pregnancy and Birth of Your Vall Pups

This is just a brief description. Most veterinarians will provide detailed information about how to handle the whelping process. If you need more information, you'll have plenty of time to copy advice of other veterinary practices available online. Plus your breeder's help will be invaluable.

Before the term "puppy" became popular in the late 1400's, "whelp" was the word for a young or newborn dog (and many other mammals). And "whelping" referred to the birthing process of a dog and was not replaced by "puppying".

Whether your bitch got pregnant by your choice or she wasn't quarantined successfully during estrus, she will give birth about two months after she was first serviced. She will eat normally until toward the end of her pregnancy when the pups really start to grow. She won't have room for her regular once or twice a day feedings so give her smaller amounts more frequently.

Keep your veterinarian informed; at a minimum he'll want to see the bitch a week or so before she's due. She could have anywhere from one to ten puppies – your vet will be able to estimate how many at this last visit.

- Gather What's Needed

Get a whelping box ready big enough for her and her pups. About four foot square with sides to block drafts on three sides. A sturdy cardboard carton is good. You can cut out one side for her to enter. Place in a quiet area of the house away from traffic. Let her get used to it well before whelping time. You can have comfortable pad and blanket up until she starts her contractions; then replace the blanket with plenty of newspapers. Keep the whelping box away from any drafts.

If she hides away and decides to have her pups somewhere else and you find her having contractions -- let her be. Don't disturb her by trying to move her, it may stop the contractions. And, while you need to observe this process, try to stay at a distance.

Get other materials ready: At a minimum you'll need clean towels, more newspapers, good scissors standing in alcohol, Betadine, nasal aspirator and dental floss. The area should be warm; have a heating pad available to warm the puppies – the bitch may not want to deal with them until all the pups are born.

- Behavior before birth

The bitch's behavior will change shortly before you can see contractions. She may refuse food and start tossing things about to make a nest. Her temperature will fall slowly a few days before she whelps.

Wash her nipples gently and look for any abnormal discharge such as green mucus or bloody milk. During the weeks she nurses keep an eye on her nipples; clean any dried milk. Report any inflammation or sensitivity to your veterinarian.

- Contractions & Births

After she begins having contractions, it may take up to two hours for the first puppy to be born. Your veterinarian will let you know at what point you should call him for help. Then each subsequent puppy can take anywhere from a few minutes to two hours to be born.

The puppy may be born inside a fluid-filled sac, or the sac may have been broken during birth. Wait for the mother break the sac, nip off the umbilical cord, and clean the puppy. If she doesn't do this, break the sac yourself, aspirate any gunk from the nose and mouth if needed, and towel off the puppy until you're sure it's breathing and moving well. Then cut the umbilical cord with your scissors.

Put a drop of Betadine at the end of each puppy's umbilical cord and tie it ¼ to ½ inch (0.6-1.3 cm) from the abdomen. The rest of the cord will dry and fall off in a few days. Then give the puppy for her to nurse. There will be an afterbirth associated with each puppy but they may not come out after each puppy – so keep a record of the number that have been expelled. Your veterinarian will want to know if one has been retained.

Your bitch may clean and nurse each puppy or wait until all the pups are born before nursing. If she's not nursing them, place them on a warming bed made by towels covering a heating pad. You want the puppy's rectal temperature to be 100 °F.

- Between puppies

Offer your bitch water or broth. She may not take it but it should be available.

When all the puppies are born take her outside to pee, clean the whelping box, and settle the family in the box.

- Care of puppies
  The puppies should be little round things that eat and sleep. They'll wriggle if you pick them up. If one seems sickly, weak, or very thin: you'll consult your veterinarian.

- Care of bitch

Watch her. If she doesn't regain her appetite, vomits, breathes abnormally, is restless, or has vaginal discharge that doesn't look right: you'll consult your veterinarian.

Chapter 31: Medicine & Your Swedish Vallhund

1. When to Call Your Veterinarian

Call your veterinarian whenever you think something is wrong with your Vallhund. I'll provide a list of some things to watch for but the best hope for your dog is that you really know her. When she's not acting like herself watch carefully for signs of illness or injury. Is she not eating? Whiny? Inactive? Look closer. Gums pale? Stools bloody?

There are situations that are clearly emergencies such as when your Vall...

- Has been hit by a car, bike, etc.

- Has been attacked by another dog, cat, or other animal – especially if puncture wound or skin tear

- Picks up one leg and won't put it back down

- Is bleeding heavily

- Is lying unconscious

- Has a seizure

- Had what you thought was a cold but now you can hear her chest gurgle

- Has a belly that's inflating, getting tight

- Is walking strangely ... wobbly, seems dizzy

- Is breathing hard for no apparent reason

- Is in acute pain, even if you can't tell what's wrong, she whines or even screams, can't get comfortable, won't let you touch her, snaps or bites.

- Has blood in stool, vomit, or from nose or ear.

- Has been left in a hot car and is breathing hard or acting dizzy

- If you investigate and her gums are pale or her temperature is either too high or too low. (Normal is 100-102.5 °F, higher after exercise; worry if 104 °F, or higher).

Then there are the less acute symptoms that should be reported; your veterinarian may just want you to watch for a day or two or make an appointment:

With your SV somewhat at risk for hip and knee problems, be sure you can identify either of these developing in your dog:

- Patella luxation: Your puppy will be examined at the breeders for a loose kneecap. If it develops later, the first sign you'll have is your dog pulls up after running and holds his foot off the ground. After a while he'll just go on as before. If this happens when he's still a puppy have your vet evaluate it. You may need to back off on the dog's activity while watching his weight.

- Hip Dysplasia: Hip dysplasia can result in arthritis and other degenerative conditions around the hip joint. You'll have a good idea of the risk of this from the data you received from the breeder about your dog's parents and grandparents. I've covered the need for you to not provide too many calories or too much calcium, especially until your dog reaches skeletal maturity; and to avoid over exercising and obesity. Later, if she develops hip problems you may notice her gait has changed and that she is lame and groans when she gets up after lying in bed -- especially after exercise. Treatment can range from pain relief to surgery.

2. Be Watchful

If someone is always around the dog you'd have a good idea if her behavior is related to an injury. Your SV may have stepped into a hole and broken her leg or her ribs may have been hurt after too much roughhousing. Pay attention to her. If she's whining and flinching if you touch her in a certain place, off to the vet!

3. Other Signs of Illness or Injury:

- Vomiting and diarrhea are common, especially when changing your dog's diet. But there should be no blood and it shouldn't go longer than a day or so, especially with a puppy. Vomiting shouldn't be explosive.

- Trying to pee very frequently; different that her usual schedule

- Cough

- You notice bruises for no reason: could be seen on her belly, ears, or in her mouth.

- Gait seems off – back legs not working the same

4. First Aid Kit

- Buy a **good first aid book** for dogs and read it before you even bring your Swedish Vallhund home. Keep it in or near your dog's first aid kit.

- You would also do well to talk about a first aid kit with your veterinarian before you even go get your puppy. What you need in your kit depends upon access to round-the-clock vet care in your area. Ideally you should have enough in your kit to be able to call the vet with a problem and then go ahead and do what she recommends.

- What should you be prepared for? Your dog may have little scrapes, insect bites, ticks, splinters, porcupine quills, skunk spraying, dog & cat bites, serious injury with heavy bleeding, injured bone, poisoning ... just to name a few.

- You can't be expected to equip yourself with an emergency room's volume of supplies, but owners of injured dogs without kits wished they'd had at least the basics. Have an elastic bandage or some other cloth or pantyhose to use as a **muzzle** if you need to attend to a wound. Have a thermometer ... it might help your vet know what's up.

- Porcupine Encounters

Some things are best treated first by your veterinarian without your intervention. If your dog gets "quilled" for example. Often a dog will get a face full of quills in its first encounter with a porcupine. Removing these quills is best done by your vet and possibly under anesthesia. Quills bury themselves deeper and deeper into the dogs flesh; if you try to pull one out, you may force others deeper.

With that caveat, if you have a good pair of **locking hemostats**, and you are miles away from help, you can remove a few quills if they are not deeply imbedded or in a cluster. Otherwise, I'd leave it for the professionals.

- Skunked

If there are skunks in your neighborhood prepare for what you'll do before it happens. There are two medical concerns: the dog's eyes can be terrible irritated by the spray, and the skunk may have bitten the dog. So, take care of the eyes first. Then de-stink the dog. And then examine it carefully for any wounds.

If you can, avoid bringing the dog inside; or if inside, put the dog in the bathroom tub with the door closed and an open window. Put on old clothes and wear latex gloves. Do not try to rinse your dog with water before using the de-stink solution.

If the dog is acting as if the spray's hurting his eyes wash the eyes with sterile saline. Ask your veterinarian whether you should then add an **eye ointment** or **mineral oil** to the eyes to protect them while you de-stink the dog.

The skunk's spray is oily and will cling to the dog's hair; you don't want to spread it around. Blot with paper towels and even cut off long hair in the sprayed area. In an open plastic bucket (a closed container will explode) add a quart of fresh (unopened) 3% **hydrogen peroxide**, ¼ cup **baking soda**, two teaspoons **liquid soap**, and a cup or two of warm water. Mix. Massage the mixture well into the sprayed area making sure you get it into your SV's undercoat. Let it stay on for ten minutes then rinse with warm water. You may have to repeat several times.

When the stink is gone, check the dog carefully for wounds. If his eyes are red or he's acting as if his eyes bother him, call your vet.

This stink removing formula was developed by a chemist, Paul Krebaum and has stood up well in competition with other methods. Drink the tomato juice yourself.

I've discussed skunking at length because almost every dog not living in the penthouse will experience this -- down at street level, skunks are common in city parks and other green areas and many cities are experiencing a growth in their skunk population. Be prepared!

Little scrapes
Just like a kid, your puppy may get scratches and nicks. A styptic pencil will stop bleeding from minor cuts or torn toenails. A spray compound such as **Vetericyn** is good to have for a wound disinfectant. If the wound is dirty, wash first, or at least flush with hydrogen peroxide.

- Bites

You're already protecting your dog against fleas, ticks and worms. When you take your dog outside there are other things that can bite and sting: wasps, bees, snakes and spiders are just a few.

My best advice is go to a good pet first aid course in your area and find out what's out there and how to deal with it.

If you live in 'tick land', add a **tick key** to your keychain so you'll always have it. The key allows you to safely remove the tick, head and all.

If your dog has had a bad reaction to a bee or wasp sting, your vet may prescribe an **Epipen** and give you instructions for its use.

- Splinters etc.

If your dog is limping inspect her feet. She may have a glass or wood splinter, a plant thorn, a wire fragment or something else stuck in her paw. Have a good pair of locking hemostats to pull these things out before they become embedded. Or use a good pair of **tweezers**. Then spray with your antibacterial spray. Keep a watch on her foot to make sure it doesn't become infected.

- Injury with heavy bleeding

It may not happen, but if it does you owe your dog to be prepared for an injury with heavy bleeding. She may have just tripped and landed on something sharp. Be ready. You may be able to stop bleeding by applying pressure on the wound. But if you can't there are materials such as **PetClot**, which will speed clotting. Supplied as a gel or in impregnated gauze, you apply directly to the wound, applying pressure. When bleeding stops, secure **gauze** with **self-adhesive wrap**. Then off to the vet.

- Poisoning

Symptoms of poisoning can range all over the place: your SV could be vomiting or drooling, have diarrhea or black tarry stools, spurn food, be weak or collapse, have yellow or pale gums. You've been warned about human foods, household plants and dangerous chemicals. If you suspect your dogs have been poisoned the biggest help you can be for the dog is to know what he's gotten into. Some poisons the vet will want you to induce vomiting, others she will not. You may be directed to do nothing yourself; just speed off to the vet. The **hydrogen peroxide** in your kit will make your dog vomit; **activated charcoal tablets** can absorb some toxins.

- What goes into your SV's first aid kit?

Be prepared! Buy a good first aid book and read it. Buy a prepackaged first aid kit for dogs and add any items in bold above which are missing from the kit.

Chapter 32: Your Senior Vallhund

Every dog ages differently – just like people do. Some Vallhunds remain sound and frisky into their teens, others are slowed by arthritis and disease by then. As your Vall becomes a senior there are steps you can take to keep him healthy.

1. Watch Him

Your Vall is not a wimp. Unless in terrible pain, he'll be slow to show it. This dog wants to work and doesn't want to get fired. He'll try to keep up even if his back and legs hurt. Changes happen slowly so you need to be alert. If he has trouble getting up in the morning; trouble getting comfortable lying down at night; limps; avoids stairs. Talk with your vet. Your dog may benefit from dietary supplements early in his 'seniorhood'; trials with glucosamine chondroitin (just do a trial – this works for some, not for others); fish oils; or anti-inflammatory meds. And now some veterinarians are finding stem cells made from the dog's fat helps about 80% of dogs treated at costs of $2,000-$5,000 (1210-3020£). (Cost often includes cells for future injections.)

As when he was a pup, watch for signs of illness which will usually be slow or abrupt changes in habits: he drinks more or less water; his appetite increases or decreases; he goes from happy self to depressed or grumpy or snippy old man dog; despite daily tooth brushing his breath stinks. Talk to your vet – these can be signs of illnesses that can be treated.

Make sure he has a good soft bed.

2. Calorie Control

He's moving less and needs fewer calories. Keep him trim. How can you tell if he's overweight? Has his collar gone up a notch or two? You veterinarian weighs him – what's been the trend. If anything he should weigh less if he's exercising less – not as much muscle. Then stand over him – behind his ribs his body should show a waist. Similarly, when looked at from the side, his belly should be tucked up behind his ribs. Feel his – they should

feel as if they're right below his skin. Compare him to old photos
– has even his face become fuller?

3. Is Your Veterinarian the Right Fit?

You need to have a vet you can ask questions to and get answers.
With the right office, you'll be eager to schedule visits twice a
year so you can catch problems early.

4. Keep up his Grooming & Meds

Brush his teeth every day. Groom his coat more if he's doing it
less. Watch for skin lumps and discolorations.

Keep up the flea, tick, and worming regimen. At some point,
especially if he's ever had a bad reaction, talk to your veterinarian
about stopping vaccinations. It's more expensive, but have
serology tests run to see if your dog already has sufficient
immunity.

5. Adapt

If he develops a bone or muscular problem so he can no longer
play his favorite sports, find something else for him to do. Try
scent tracking for instance – it'll be good for his brain and
psyche. Does he like to swim? Find a pool. Don't forget the
games you taught him as a puppy ... hide his favorite toy, find the
treat, low impact fetch inside.

Watch out for over exercising him. Go for three or four outings a
day rather than one long hike.

At some point your Vall may have difficulty hearing or seeing. In
your earlier training be sure to use hand and voice commands
together.

At some point your dear Vall may not be able to make it through
the night. Set up a pee pad in a low plastic pan some place
convenient for him.

Some dogs lose their coordination such that walking on hard
floors is difficult. They still do well on rugs. Make it easy for him
– add some floor runners so he can move around easily.

Chapter 33: Your Vall's Last Days

As your dog ages, you'll think of her dying, you can't help it. Most dogs do not die in their sleep or die suddenly. Unless they are killed in an accident, they – as humans do – die from a myriad of illnesses. About a third of adult dog deaths are from cancer; 10% from trauma; 7% from infections. Toward the very end of their life, a dog's cause of death may be recorded as being from old age – this is when the dog has many organs, which are simply not working.

Over its history, veterinary medicine has made many diseases preventable or treatable. Now, it has also evolved to offer more heroic and expensive diagnostic and treatment options, which may stun and bewilder the pet owner. This makes it essential that you have a veterinarian you can trust to give you a full picture of your dog's illness.

There are often more options than some veterinarians want to give you. You must press for as much information as you need. Is the treatment a cure? How much longer will she live? What will be the quality of her life after the treatment? How much will it cost? If I can't afford to do the veterinarian's preferred option, what else can I do for her? I have pet insurance, how much of the cost will be covered?

After any and all medical treatments, most Vall owners will have to decide whether to let their dog die "naturally", to have some hospice care, or to have it euthanized. Some things to consider:

- If your dog was in pain, can her pain be controlled? (Dogs don't usually yelp or cry from pain; they withdraw, and their heart rate and blood pressure increases).

- Does she have bowel and bladder control? Always/Usually/Sometimes/Never?

- Is your dog still eating well? Is she drinking water? Or does she need an IV to stay alive?

- Can she still walk enough to reach her bowls and puppy pad?

- Is she happy to see you? Does her tail still wag? Does she still chew her toys? Or are her eyes dull and show no interest in you or anyone or anything else.

- Are her good days still more than her bad ones?

- Is she seizing or walking in circles?

As you evaluate each part of her life, the picture will become clear over time.

You have to decide what's best for your dog. Dog's live for the day. Is she happy to see the day?

1. Hospice

A visit from a hospice veterinarian may clarify your situation. While you may not be able to afford long-term hospice care, having another professional evaluate your dog's condition could help. Your dog may be better off than you thought. There may be ways to make your dog more comfortable for a period of time. Or the hospice veterinarian can give you peace of mind that you've done all you could and it is not being kind to the dog to keep it alive any longer.

Pet owners are generally afraid to euthanize a dog too soon – until afterward when they often feel guilt they've let the dog be miserable for too long.

In performing euthanasia, a catheter is placed in the dog's vein, usually in a forearm. You can pet her and talk with her and cry. If your dog still likes treats, you can feed her favorites. When you're ready the veterinarian will inject an overdose of anesthetic. Your dog will become limp and die within 10-20 seconds.

You can decide where euthanasia is done. Some prefer to be at home, so the dog doesn't have to be moved. If your own veterinarian won't make a house call there are others who will. Many owners bring their dogs to the veterinarians, but don't go inside. Their dog loves the ride. Then the veterinarian comes out and does the injection in the vehicle. Other dogs love to go to the veterinarian and some offices even have a nice room for this.

2. What To Do with Your Vall's Body

- Bury in the back yard. If you own your home (and plan to live in it "forever", you can bury your dog in most communities. Your state or community may have laws about how deep you need to bury her and how far away from water sources.

- Bury in pet cemetery. Even if there is no pet cemetery in your community, many of them will pick up your dog for burial. Be careful in choosing the service; some small services stop accepting new pets after a few years and no longer care for the property. Cemeteries usually offer a wide range of services, from simple burial costing $300-$500 (180-300£) to a full human-type ceremony for which some owners spend $7,000 (4225£) or more.

- Cremate – communal. In communal cremation, your dog will be cremated with other animals. Some crematoriums provide the mixed ashes later; some don't provide ashes. Costs vary, some charitable organization provide euthanasia and cremation for $50 (30£) or so. Cremation for a Vallhund ranges from $50 to $150 (30-90£).

- Cremate – individual. Your dog is cremated by itself and her ashes are returned to you. The ashes may be in a simple cardboard box for scattering or a wooden box or metal urn for saving. $200-$350 (120-210£), plus cost of box or urn.

- City Waste Disposal – In some cities, like New York City, you may place your dog on the curb for the regular city waste pickup. You must place her in a black plastic bag on pickup day and put a tag on it that it is a dead dog inside. If the pickup isn't scheduled within a day, you need to keep the bag on ice or in a freezer.

- Taxidermy – Not all dogs are suitable for taxidermy. If sick for a long time the dog's coat may not accept the procedure. There are two methods used: the traditional way, with a mold made and the cleaned skin applied to it or the freeze-dry method in which the body is posed and then slowly frozen under vacuum to remove all the water. Some companies want the body frozen right away and shipped overnight to begin the process. Other companies take the body and store it frozen for some time for you reconsider your decision. Costs can be high, vary by community, and can range from $1,000-$3,000 (600-1810£).

3. Grief

Let yourself grieve for your Vallhund. Don't let anyone do the "it's just a dog" bit. People react differently. Your kids may wail for a few days and then go on while you are hit by waves of sadness over the loss for weeks or months.

I've found it helpful to bury my dog myself; somehow the digging, then wrapping my dog in a sheet or towel and lowering her into the ground is soothing. Putting the dirt back. Finding rocks to cover the hole so animals won't try to dig her up. Then later planting something over her – usually a plant she would have loved to destroy. All of that soothes me. If you have kids, you can have a nice ceremony and they can all help.

Scattering ashes or keeping them at home also presents opportunities for ceremony and reflection about your good dog.

I'm not attracted to taxidermy, but that's just me. Would I then bury the dog with me when I die? And I'm afraid it would just extend my sadness when I saw her every day. But others are comforted by having their dog with them always.

4. When to Have Another Dog

Whether and when to have another dog is a totally personal decision. I've found many people firmly state never to have another dog then see one on TV at the local pound and go right off and take one in. Others change breeds, or species. One way to see if you're ready for a dog is to do fostering of shelter pets. Fostering is also an alternative for the elderly who reason they would outlive another Vallhund and wouldn't want to desert their dog.

Chapter 34: The Law, You, and Your SV

My intent here is just to show you where the potholes may be. There are so many dog laws out there as well as other legal situations dog owners find themselves in that I thought it worthwhile to discuss a few.

1. Agreements and Contracts

Be careful what you sign. If you go to rent an apartment in a "no pets allowed" building and the landlord assures you that this doesn't apply to your sweet little Vallhund: don't sign his regular lease. Have it changed, or change it yourself, to add that Sigmund may live there as long as you promise to clean up the yard after him, or pay for cleaning when you leave, etc.

You'll get a copy of the contract proposed by breeders for your pet (with spay/neuter clause and maybe co-owner clause) or your show or breeder dog (with co-owner provisions) – it wouldn't hurt to run them by an attorney.

Your dog is lost and found by someone who won't return it. Your roommate/spouse/partner breaks up with you and takes the dog. Your dog is stolen and you've discovered where he is. There is a legal recourse (replevin) so you can have the dog returned fairly quickly if you have some proof of ownership. Permanent proof of ownership may be required at a hearing. So think. Who does own the dog and can you prove it? Proof that you bought the dog in your name; was the one taking it to the veterinarian and dog park; paid for his food, etc.

Your will. Dogs are considered property so in the old days people who left money to the pets had their wills overturned. Now, however, establishing a Pet Trust in your will is possible in most areas. The Pet Trust owns some of your property and the trustee uses it to pay for your dog's care. The beneficiary cares for the dog and may also receive some payment for doing so. Often when the dog dies the remaining trust funds are given to an animal charity. A trust provides you with greater assurance that your dog will be cared for. If you have a trusted friend you can simply bequeath the dog and some funds to her – but if something happens to her...

2. A Sample of Laws

If you are elderly or handicapped and live in government funded housing in the US you have certain rights to own a pet.

If you bring a pet onto a US Federal Wildlife Area, get a copy of their dog policy and obey the rules. There are harsh penalties if your dog kills wildlife or is found running loose.

If you plan to breed a dog, check your area's laws. In a few US states you must be a licensed breeder just to have one litter. Some cities require most pets be spayed or neutered.

Many areas require confinement of bitches in heat.

Many areas have limits on the number of dogs you may own.

Most areas require rabies vaccination.

Many areas, including Australia and New Zealand require microchipping.

Loose dogs. Find out what the policy is on different areas – especially around livestock and in parks. Every area is different. In Kentucky, a dog running loose between sundown and sunrise may be killed by law enforcement unless suspected of being a lost hunting dog.

Many area permit shooting a dog in pursuit of wildlife or livestock.

Driving. It's against the law in some areas to drive with your dog on your lap. It's also against the law in many areas for a dog to be in an open truck bed or vehicle without being tied or crated.

Leash laws are almost everywhere; or at least laws that require the dog to be under your control.

Dangerous dog laws are prevalent. Some focus on acts of the dog – biting, threatening. Others are breed-specific which does not concern Vall owners.

Many areas have laws for housing your dog. How long you can tether him to a solid object ... a post, doghouse etc. and how long the tether must be. How long you can keep him outside, or hours you cannot keep him outside. Fencing required. Water and food requirements if left outside.

Most areas have dog cruelty laws.

Dog bites: If your dog bites someone you can be sued. In some areas no account is made for the actions of the victim – teasing, taunting, etc. Dogs no longer get one free bite in most areas. Many areas require the bite be reported to the health department. This report can end up with your dog becoming a dangerous dog. Handling of dangerous dogs varies widely by area, ranging from euthanasia, quarantine or muzzling in public.

Nuisance laws, barking laws. Check your community's laws concerning barking or nuisances. If you live in a dense suburban area and your dog spends time in your backyard and you aren't tidy or your dog barks at all hours, you could end up in court. If a neighbor complains, take him seriously. See how you can change your or your dog's behavior. In Berkeley CA, an owner of a problem barking dog can rent an anti-barking collar from the Berkeley Dispute Resolution Center.

3. License

Finally, most areas require your dog to have a license. Your veterinarian will know the procedure for obtaining a dog license in your municipality.

In the US, dog licenses can be based upon state, county, or municipal laws. Most require proof of rabies vaccination. Fees vary, often lower if the dog is spayed or neutered or if it is a service dog. Fines are usually the penalty for not licensing your dog. Many states and municipalities also have laws restricting dangerous breeds and dangerous dogs. It is possible that your Swedish Vallhund could be considered a dangerous dog if someone reported it biting or threatening.

Great Britain stopped its dog licensing requirement in 1987 as it was unenforceable. In 1991 the Dangerous Dogs Act established strict rules for four "types" of dogs: pit bull terrier, Japanese Tosa, Dogo Argentino and Fila Brasileiro. The Act requires court approval to even own one of these dogs; breeding is prohibited.

Northern Ireland requires licensure.

Australia has laws similar to the US, with licenses required and fees varied by municipality. Victoria has special laws for menacing or dangerous dogs as well as restricted breed laws. Menacing or dangerous dogs are those which have bitten or threatened someone or who guard buildings with no owner present; these dogs must wear red and yellow striped dog collars.

New Zealand now require microchipping as part of their licensing requirements.

Summary

The Swedish Vallhund is a rare breed. I've attempted in this book to give you a full idea of the enjoyment you can have with your Vallhund as well as the responsibilities you assume by owning one. I've tried throughout to give a frank picture of the costs and efforts needed to train your dog well and keep her mentally and physically healthy. If you become a Vallhund owner, I wish both of you a long and enjoyable life!

Appendix A: Pre-purchase agreement

(March 2014)

Full name **(Required)**

_____

1. Your occupation?

_____

2. Spouse / Companion occupation?

_____

3. What type of residence do you live in?

_____

4. Do you rent or own?

_____

5. Do you have children under the age of 12?

_____

6. How did you hear about XSBaggage Swedish Vallhunds?

7. If given a referral, please tell us who referred you?

_____

8. Do you have a fenced yard?

_____

9. If not, how will you provide security for your puppy when it is outside or when you are away?

10. What sex of puppy would you prefer? Male __Female__

11. Would you consider a puppy of the opposite sex if your preference were not available? Yes _____No_____

12. What color are you interested in? _____

13. Would you consider a puppy of another color if your color preference were not available? Yes___ No___

14. When are you ready to add a Swedish Vallhund to your household? _____

15. For what purpose are you interested in a Swedish Vallhund? (i.e. pet, show, or breeding)

_____

16. Have you read any literature on the Swedish Vallhund? Do you understand that the breed has possible health/behavioral issues? (i.e. eyes, hips) There is no way

to tell if your future family companion will be affected during his/her lifetime. A twelve months guarantee is given, if for some reason your future pet develops a fatal/hereditary condition, a 25% refund is negotiable.(Note: A veterinary document must support findings) *Do you fully understand and agree with this?*
Yes _____ No _____

17. Is someone home during the day, or able to get home for the puppy to potty? _____

18. Are you familiar with crate training? _____

19. How long will the puppy be left unattended during the day?

20. Where will the puppy sleep?
_____

21. Are you willing to attend group-training classes with the puppy?

22. Have you owned herding breed before?
_____

23. If not, what types of dog(s) have you owned?
_____

24. Do you still own the dog(s)? _____

25. If not, what happened to the dog(s)? _____

26. Please give name, address, and telephone number of your Veterinarian (or one that has worked with you in the past) I will be contacting the Veterinarian for a reference in regards to past animal care.

27. Do you agree that puppy is to have yearly vaccines, eyes checked by an ophthalmologist . Yes _____ No _____

28. Who will have primary responsibility for care of the puppy? _____

29. Are you interested in showing? _____

30. Are you interested in breeding? _____

31. What qualities do you like about the Swedish Vallhund?
_____

32. Do you understand that Swedish Vallhunds can be difficult to train, largely because they are motivated

differently from most other breeds?
_____

33. What are your preferences in dog food for your dog/puppy? _____

34. The cost of an XSBaggage Swedish Vallhund puppy is $1400.00, if puppy is sold for pet it must be spayed/neutered at 6 mos. of age. This does not include transport expenses. Do you agree with this? Yes_____ No_____

35. A $500.00 "In good faith" deposit is required once a person/family is approved. If a puppy of your selection is not available, you have two options: Receive a full refund or be placed on the waiting list for the next available litter. Do you agree with this? Yes_____ No_____

36. Once a decision is made to approve/disapprove you for a XSBaggage Swedish Vallhund puppy. You will be contacted, and notified that you'll be put on the waiting list. You will then have 7 days from the time approved to send your $500.00 "good faith" deposit. If the deposit is not received in the allotted time, you will be removed from the waiting list. Do you agree with this? Yes_____ No_____

37. Once puppies are born, the purchaser will be responsible for paying the remaining balance two weeks after the birth of your puppy. In addition, if you request that your future puppy requires transport, the cost of airfare will be determined by the airport destination. Do you agree with this?
Yes _____ No _____

38. I would like buyer(s) to keep in mind, if for any reason you cannot keep the puppy/dog. XSBaggage Swedish Vallhunds reserves the right to have the puppy/dog sent back at the buyer(s) expense with no refund available. **At no time will consent be given for the puppy/dog to be resold or given away.** Do you agree with this?
Please initial: Yes _____ No_____

39. You agree to use XSBaggage in the front of the puppy's name in registration and any advertising will use the full registered name:
Yes _____ No _____

Do you agree with Questionnaire/Agreement? If so, please acknowledge by signing below.
Buyer(s) Signatures:
_____

Thank you for your interest in our wonderful breed! We are happy to help you with any questions you have. Please return this completed form: one copy via email attachment and a hand written copy by mail, both methods are preferred.

XSBaggage Swedish Vallhunds
40115 NE 174th Ave
Amboy WA 98601

Appendix B: Swedish Vallhund Videos

These are just a few of my favorites. There are lots more out there to choose from. Enjoy!

Search for these videos on Youtube.com

Fun to Watch on YouTube

Basil the Swedish Vallhund is One!
Clips of Basil romping in the ocean, at home, with other dogs

Agility World Championships 2009: WCO9 team Niina-Liina and Rhett
Video is a little fuzzy but demonstrates the amazing speed of the Swedish Vallhund

Vallhund Face Skiing
Funny

Intelligence is a Swedish Vallhund
Dog comes in wet from a walk. Antics to try to dry itself is hilarious. Good demo of the dog's energy

Swedish Vallhund Walking
Three-year-old Vallhund walking a puppy on a leash
You can train this dog to do almost anything

Swedish Vallhund Footballing Legend !!!
Dog show sremarkable control of the soccer ball

Mission impossible
Funny story with a Vallhund travelling to the butchers to steal a recipe for sausage

Hygiene

Cleaning dog teeth with electric toothbrush - Honey the Great Dane

How to Clip Dog Nails - Tips from the Dog Training Guys (k9-1.com)
Good way to remember the angle of the cut you want -- Indian in canoe

How to Clean Your Dog's Ears - VetVid Episode 003
Veterinarian show how clean dog's ear.

Training

Dog Pulling Or Fighting The Leash, Problems Walking Dog
One of zillions of how to walk your dog on a leash

Basic Clicker Training Equipment
Donna Hill
Basic description of clickers, best treats, etc.

Getting Started with Clicker Training
Donna Hill
Basic How-To -- Teaching dog to make eye contact

Putting a Dog's Unwanted Behavior on Stimulus Control (To Get Rid of it)
Donna Hill
Dog jumped on woman whenever she put the food down for him. So she trained him to jump on cue. Then lessened the cues until the dog stopped jumping on her

Sports

Treibball bei der DogLive Gala 2012
A Tribball game (audio in German)

Appendix C: Selected Web Sites

Vallhund Sites for Samples of Breed Standards

The Kennel Club
www.thekennelclub.org.uk

www.akc.org
American Kennel Club

www.fci.be
FCI - Fédération Cynologique Internationale

Other Selected Vallhund Sites

www.svak.se
Svenska Vallhundsklubben SVAK
and
www.skk.se
Svenska Kennelklubben
Sweden's Vallhund and Kennel Clubs: Good source of info,
including breeder contracts. Much of the sites is in English. Use
Google as search engine and it's translate the rest.

www.vasgotaspets.com
Site of Australian/New Zealand enthusiasts
Excellent information on history/anatomy/literature/puppy
care/litters available/FGF5 genetics. Has links to breeders
worldwide.

www.swedishvallhund.com
Site for the American Swedish Vallhund Club.
Has a breeders list and information about their rescue program

www.swedishvallhunds.co.uk
Site for UK Swedish Vallhund club.

General breed information. Links to breeders. Interesting note on tail genetics.

www.swedishvallhundclubofcanada.com
Site of Canada's Vallhund club
Canada breed standard and links to breeders

www.swedishvallhunds.co.uk
Swedish Vallhund Society UK
Good discussion bobtail genetics

General Dog Sites

www.akc.org
American Kennel Club
Good materials for competition rules and training for them

http://animallaw.info
Animal Legal & Historical Center
Michigan University College of Law
Has US state dog laws and other information/discussion

Western Australian Laws Relating to Dogs
Nov 14, 2013 ... Your legal rights and responsibilities are outlined in the Dog Act 1976, the Dog Regulations 2013, and in local government local laws.
www.dlg.wa.gov.au
Has copies of dog laws for each community

www.aspca.org
ASPCA | Official Site for the American Society for the Prevention of Cruelty to Animals
Good resource for human foods poisonous to dogs; other poisons; list with photos of plants that are poisonous plus list of common plants that aren't toxic to dogs.

Viking & Swedish Names

www.angelfire.com
A collation of Viking names by Stephen Francis Wyley

www.babynames.org.uk/swedish-baby-names.htm
A list of Swedish first names with their meaning

Published by IMB Publishing 2014